Modern Excel Automatic

Migrating VBA Macros to Office Scri
Automate

Modern Excel Automation:

Migrating VBA Macros to Office Scripts and Power Automate

Modern Excel Automation:

Migrating VBA Macros to Office Scripts and Power Automate

Modern Excel Automation:

Migrating VBA Macros to Office Scripts and Power Automate

Modern Excel Automation:

Migrating VBA Macros to Office Scripts and Power Automate

Modern Excel Automation:

Migrating VBA Macros to Office Scripts and Power Automate

1. Introduction to Modern Excel Automation

For decades, Excel has been the cornerstone of data analysis, reporting, and everyday business tasks. What began as a simple spreadsheet application has evolved into a powerful platform capable of sophisticated automation and integration with cloud-based tools. In the past, most automation within Excel relied on VBA macros—snippets of code written to streamline repetitive tasks, manipulate data, and build interactive reports. These macros became a lifeline for power users and developers, weaving themselves into the daily operations of countless organizations.

However, the digital landscape is shifting. As businesses embrace the flexibility and accessibility of the cloud, Microsoft has reimagined how Excel fits into a modern, connected workflow. Excel Online, together with new technologies like Office Scripts and Power Automate, is opening the door to a new era of automation—one that is accessible, scalable, and collaborative. These tools aren't just replacing VBA; they are redefining what's possible.

Modern Excel automation is no longer confined to a single desktop or a lone power user's expertise. It's about creating smart, cloud-based processes that respond in real time, work across applications, and can be managed by teams instead of individuals. This shift brings enormous potential—but it also requires a new mindset. Learning how to transition from VBA to Office Scripts, and understanding how to use Power Automate to orchestrate workflows across Microsoft

365, is becoming essential for those who want to stay ahead in the world of data and automation.

Whether you're a longtime Excel expert or just starting to explore the world of scripting and automation, this book is here to guide you through the transition. We'll help you understand not only how these new tools work, but why they matter—and how they can make your daily work more efficient, secure, and future-ready.

To begin this journey, we'll take a closer look at where it all started—with a chapter exploring **The Evolution of Excel Macros: From Desktop to Cloud**.

The Evolution of Excel Macros: From Desktop to Cloud

The story of Excel macros begins in the early days of desktop computing, when automation meant writing lines of VBA code directly within a local Excel workbook. For many users, VBA—Visual Basic for Applications—was a revelation. It empowered analysts, accountants, and developers to go beyond formulas and pivot tables, building custom solutions that saved hours of manual work. With just a few clicks, tasks like cleaning data, generating reports, and sending emails could be performed instantly and consistently. VBA became a silent hero in offices around the world, embedded in templates, financial models, and workflow systems.

For years, this approach worked beautifully. But the world changed. As organizations moved toward cloud-based collaboration and remote work, a new challenge emerged: traditional macros didn't fit well into this new environment. VBA macros are tightly bound to desktop Excel. They can't run in Excel Online, they aren't easily shareable in cloud workspaces, and they often struggle with compatibility in modern Microsoft 365 environments. Security concerns also became more pressing, as VBA files could contain potentially harmful code, leading to stricter controls and frequent blocks on macro-enabled workbooks.

Meanwhile, Microsoft began investing heavily in cloud-native tools designed for modern workflows. Excel Online emerged as a powerful platform in its own right, no longer just a viewer but a full-featured application. Alongside it came Office Scripts—a new scripting language built specifically for Excel on the web. With JavaScript at its core and designed for automation in cloud environments, Office Scripts opened the door to a new kind of macro: one that is portable, secure, and designed for team-based collaboration. Add to that the capabilities of Power Automate, and suddenly automation isn't just about Excel—it's about connecting Excel to an entire ecosystem of apps and services.

This shift doesn't mean VBA is obsolete. On the contrary, it's still a vital part of countless legacy systems. But as the business world leans further into the cloud, the need to migrate and modernize is becoming more urgent. Understanding how and why to make that transition is essential for any Excel user who wants to remain effective in the years ahead.

That's exactly where we're headed next, as we explore **Why Migrate from VBA to Office Scripts?**

Why Migrate from VBA to Office Scripts?

Change is never easy—especially when it involves moving away from tools that have served us well for decades. VBA has long been the engine behind Excel automation, trusted by countless users to solve real-world problems efficiently.

Modern Excel Automation:

Migrating VBA Macros to Office Scripts and Power Automate

For many, writing a macro in VBA became second nature, a dependable way to simplify tasks, eliminate repetition, and gain deeper control over their spreadsheets. It worked—and in many cases, it still does.

But the landscape of work has shifted. Businesses are now operating in increasingly cloud-based, collaborative environments, where accessibility, real-time editing, and cross-platform compatibility are no longer optional—they're essential. In this new era, traditional VBA shows its limitations. It doesn't run in Excel Online, making it incompatible with many modern workflows. Sharing and deploying VBA across teams and organizations can be complex and prone to issues. And as security standards tighten, macros are more frequently disabled by default, creating friction and frustration for users.

Office Scripts, by contrast, were designed with the future in mind. Built for Excel on the web, they offer a streamlined, secure, and cloud-ready approach to automation. Written in TypeScript, a modern and well-supported language, Office Scripts allow users to create, save, and run scripts directly within Excel Online. They work seamlessly with Power Automate, enabling workflows that stretch far beyond spreadsheets—triggered by events, scheduled in the cloud, or integrated with other Microsoft 365 apps. This shift not only makes automation more accessible to a broader audience, but also more powerful and adaptable to evolving business needs.

Migrating to Office Scripts doesn't mean abandoning the skills and logic learned through VBA—it means building on them. Many concepts carry over, and the mindset of problem-solving through code remains the same. The real difference lies in the environment: one that is collaborative, scalable, and integrated into the wider Microsoft ecosystem.

Modern Excel Automation:

Migrating VBA Macros to Office Scripts and Power Automate

It's a move that not only keeps your automation relevant but unlocks entirely new possibilities.

To understand just how powerful this ecosystem can be, we now turn to the next chapter: **Overview of Excel Online and the Power Automate Ecosystem**.

Overview of Excel Online and the Power Automate Ecosystem

Excel Online is no longer a stripped-down version of its desktop counterpart. Over the past few years, it has grown into a full-featured, dynamic platform that's deeply integrated with the Microsoft 365 ecosystem. Accessible from anywhere, on any device, Excel Online offers a modern, collaborative experience that aligns perfectly with how we work today. It allows teams to co-edit workbooks in real time, ensures documents are always up to date, and provides a seamless connection to cloud storage through OneDrive and SharePoint. But what truly sets it apart is its ability to support automation at scale—something that wasn't possible in the same way with traditional desktop Excel.

At the heart of this modern automation framework is Power Automate. This cloud-based service acts as a powerful orchestrator, connecting Excel with hundreds of other applications and services, both within and outside the Microsoft ecosystem. With Power Automate, you can design workflows that trigger when data in a spreadsheet changes, schedule reports to run automatically, send notifications, update databases, or even integrate with third-party services like Teams, Outlook, and SharePoint. And when combined with Office Scripts, these flows become even more intelligent—capable of reading, editing, and analyzing spreadsheet content in real time, all without user intervention.

The beauty of this ecosystem lies in its flexibility. Whether you're automating a simple task or designing a multi-step business process, Excel Online and Power Automate provide the tools to make it happen—all within a secure, cloud-native environment. You're no longer tied to a single machine or dependent on local files. Your scripts, flows, and data live in the cloud, accessible anytime, and ready to adapt as your needs evolve.

This powerful combination is changing the way Excel is used, especially by professionals who rely on data to make decisions, automate operations, or deliver insights faster. It brings together the familiarity of Excel with the limitless potential of automation.

As we move forward, it's worth asking: who stands to benefit most from this transformation? In the next chapter, we'll take a closer look at **Who This Book Is For**, and explore how Excel power users, analysts, and IT professionals can make the most of modern Excel automation.

Who This Book Is For

This book is written for those who see Excel as more than just a spreadsheet tool—for those who use it as a daily companion in problem-solving, reporting, analysis, and automation. Whether you've been building VBA macros for years or are just starting to explore what's possible with scripts and workflows, this guide is meant to help you take the next step in your automation journey.

If you're an Excel power user, you already understand the value of automating repetitive tasks to save time and reduce errors. This book will show you how to translate those skills into the modern, cloud-connected world of Office Scripts and Power Automate. If you're a data analyst or business professional working across teams, it will help you build workflows that are easy to share, manage, and scale. And if you're in IT or a support role, you'll learn how to help your organization adopt future-ready automation strategies that are secure, maintainable, and aligned with Microsoft's evolving platform.

No matter your background, the goal of this book is to make the transition from VBA to modern Excel automation clear, practical, and rewarding. You'll find real-world examples, best practices, and explanations that bridge the gap between what you already know and what you'll soon be able to do.

Now that we've explored who this book is for and the environment we're working in, it's time to take a deeper look at the core technologies themselves. In the next chapter, we'll begin by **Comparing VBA and Office Scripts**— examining how their architectures differ, how functionality and security compare in desktop versus online Excel, and what Microsoft's roadmap tells us about the future of both platforms.

2. Comparing VBA and Office Scripts

As Excel evolves, so too must the tools we use to automate it. For years, VBA has been the standard for creating macros in Excel. It provided users with a powerful, flexible way to automate virtually anything—from formatting cells and manipulating data to building interactive dashboards and complex logic-driven reports. With VBA, automation felt personal and precise, tailored to the nuances of each workbook and the specific needs of its creator. It gave users a sense of control and creativity that made Excel more than just a spreadsheet—it became a development platform.

But times have changed. The rise of cloud computing, remote collaboration, and cross-platform access has redefined what users expect from their tools. Office Scripts emerged in response to this shift, offering a modern alternative built for Excel Online. Rather than being tied to a single user's desktop, Office Scripts live in the cloud. They are accessible from anywhere, easy to manage, and designed to integrate with broader workflows through Power Automate. This isn't just a technical change—it's a philosophical one. Automation is no longer an isolated activity. It's now part of a larger, connected ecosystem that brings people, data, and systems together.

Comparing VBA and Office Scripts isn't about declaring a winner. It's about understanding the strengths and limitations of each approach—and recognizing where they shine in today's Excel environment. While VBA is deeply embedded in many legacy solutions and offers unmatched control on the desktop, Office Scripts provide a forward-looking path that emphasizes scalability, security, and collaboration. Both have their place, but choosing the right tool for the job depends on context, goals, and the environment in which you work.

To make this comparison clearer, let's begin by examining the core architectural differences between these two technologies. In the next section, we'll explore the foundations of **Desktop VBA and Cloud Office Scripts**, and how those foundations shape what each tool can do.

Architecture Differences (Desktop VBA vs. Cloud Office Scripts)

Understanding the architectural foundations of VBA and Office Scripts is key to appreciating how these two automation tools operate—and why they feel so different in practice. VBA was designed in an era when software lived almost entirely on individual machines. Its architecture is tightly bound to the Excel desktop application, and it runs within the context of that application. This means it has deep access to the workbook, the user interface, and even the operating system, allowing it to interact with files, folders, and other applications installed on the same machine. It's a powerful and flexible setup, but one that comes with limitations in today's connected, cloud-first world.

Office Scripts, by contrast, were built from the ground up for the cloud. Scripts are written in TypeScript, a modern, browser-friendly programming language that runs in a secure, sandboxed environment within Excel Online. The script doesn't operate inside your local machine—it operates through a cloud-based execution engine that interprets the instructions and performs actions on the workbook stored in OneDrive or SharePoint. This architecture makes Office Scripts more secure, more scalable, and more portable across devices and users. It also means that automations are not tied to a single user's environment, but can be executed from anywhere, often as part of larger workflows in Power Automate.

This shift in architecture reflects a broader change in how we think about Excel automation. Rather than being confined to the local desktop, scripts can now live in the cloud, be triggered by events, scheduled to run at specific times, or launched as part of multi-step business processes. The trade-off is that Office Scripts don't have the same level of deep system access as VBA—but what they lose in system-level control, they more than make up for in reach, security, and integration.

Now that we've explored the architectural contrasts between VBA and Office Scripts, let's take a closer look at how they compare in terms of **Functionality and Security in Excel Desktop vs. Excel Online**.

Functionality and Security in Excel Desktop vs. Excel Online

Excel has long been known for its rich feature set, and with the evolution from desktop to cloud, that functionality has only expanded—though in different ways, depending on the platform. Excel Desktop remains the most powerful version in terms of raw capabilities. It offers full support for VBA, advanced charting tools, Power Pivot, and a broad range of third-party add-ins. Users can create complex models, interact with system files, and build custom applications entirely within the Excel environment. This level of control is ideal for tasks that require deep system integration or highly customized user interactions.

Excel Online, on the other hand, is designed for accessibility, collaboration, and integration. While it doesn't yet match the desktop version feature for feature, it's catching up quickly—and in some areas, it's redefining how Excel is used. Its real-time co-authoring, cloud storage integration, and seamless link to Office Scripts and Power Automate make it a hub for connected work. Excel Online favors consistency and security over total control, meaning it operates within a sandboxed environment that protects both the user and the organization from potential vulnerabilities.

Security has become a defining factor in the shift toward cloud-based solutions. Traditional VBA macros have long been a target for malicious actors, which has led to increasingly strict security policies in many workplaces. Macros are often blocked by default, flagged by antivirus software, or disabled by IT departments altogether. Office Scripts avoid many of these issues by design. Stored and run within the Microsoft 365 cloud, they're governed by role-based permissions and organization-wide policies, making them inherently safer and easier to manage at scale. They also reduce the risks associated with sharing files, since the logic resides in the cloud rather than in the file itself.

While the desktop version of Excel continues to offer unparalleled depth for individual users, the cloud version opens new doors for collaboration, mobility, and enterprise-level governance. Choosing between them isn't always about which is better—it's about which is better suited to your specific needs and environment.

Now that we've explored how functionality and security differ across platforms, it's time to examine how automation strategies themselves have changed. In the next section, we'll look at **Automation Strategies: Event-Driven Macros vs. Cloud-Based Flows**, and how these two approaches shape the way we automate in modern Excel.

Automation Strategies: Event-Driven Macros vs. Cloud-Based Flows

Automation in Excel has always been about making work faster, easier, and more reliable. With VBA, that typically meant creating event-driven macros—scripts triggered by specific actions within the workbook. These might include opening a file, changing a cell value, or clicking a custom button embedded in a worksheet. The beauty of this approach lies in its immediacy: the code runs the moment the event occurs, offering instant feedback and a responsive user experience. For many, these types of automations became second nature, woven deeply into the daily rhythm of spreadsheet work.

As Excel moved into the cloud, a new style of automation emerged—one that's not limited to what happens within the boundaries of a single file. Cloud-based flows, powered by Office Scripts and Power Automate, take a broader view. Instead of reacting only to in-app events, they can be scheduled, triggered by external systems, or launched by user input across platforms. This shift allows automations to become part of larger business processes, stretching far beyond Excel itself. A script might update a report when a SharePoint list changes, send an alert when a specific value appears in a workbook, or archive data on a recurring schedule—all without needing the user to open Excel at all.

The flexibility of cloud-based flows changes how we think about automation. Rather than responding only to what's happening in a single file, workflows can be designed to manage data across applications, streamline collaboration, and ensure tasks happen at the right time, every time. This also makes automation more inclusive—teams can build, monitor, and share flows without needing deep programming skills, thanks to Power Automate's visual interface and integration with common apps.

Still, each approach has its place. Event-driven macros remain ideal for highly interactive Excel environments where users need immediate results based on specific actions. Cloud-based flows, meanwhile, shine when you need scale, security, and connectivity across systems. Together, they form a toolkit that supports every level of automation—from the local to the enterprise.

As organizations look to the future, many are wondering what role VBA will continue to play—and how Office Scripts will evolve alongside it. In the next section, we'll explore **Microsoft's Roadmap: The Future of VBA and Office Scripts**, to better understand where both technologies are headed.

Microsoft's Roadmap: The Future of VBA and Office Scripts

The conversation around VBA and Office Scripts isn't just about what exists today—it's also about where Microsoft is heading. For many users and organizations, understanding the long-term vision is just as important as learning the tools themselves. VBA has been part of the Excel ecosystem for over two decades, and despite the rise of new technologies, Microsoft has continued to support it. But support and innovation are not the same. While VBA still works and remains vital for legacy solutions, it's clear that future investment is leaning toward cloud-based, scalable, and secure alternatives.

Office Scripts represent Microsoft's response to the demands of modern work. As organizations move to Microsoft 365 and adopt more flexible, cloud-first environments, the need for automation that can operate across systems, devices, and users has grown rapidly. Office Scripts, especially when paired with Power Automate, fulfill that need. Microsoft is actively enhancing the Office Scripts platform—adding new features, improving compatibility, and deepening its integration with the broader Microsoft 365 ecosystem. This forward momentum signals a strong commitment to making Office Scripts the centerpiece of Excel automation in the cloud.

That said, Microsoft is not abandoning VBA. Instead, they're allowing both technologies to coexist—for now. This approach gives users time to transition, adapt, and modernize their workflows at a pace that fits their business needs. Still, the writing on the wall is clear: organizations that want to future-proof their automation strategies would be wise to begin exploring Office Scripts and Power Automate today.

To make the most of what Office Scripts has to offer, it's essential to get hands-on experience. In the next chapter, we'll walk through **Setting Up Your Office Scripts Environment**, including the tools you need, how to enable the feature in Excel Online, and how to write and run your very first script.

3. Setting Up Your Office Scripts Environment

Before diving into the world of Office Scripts, it's important to ensure you have the right environment set up. Unlike traditional Excel macros that run locally on a desktop, Office Scripts are designed to operate in the cloud. This means your tools, your data, and even your automation logic live online—accessible from anywhere, anytime. It's a new way of working with Excel, and the setup reflects that shift. Once configured properly, you'll unlock a powerful space where automation is not only possible but also seamless, collaborative, and secure.

Getting started with Office Scripts doesn't require a deep background in programming. What it does require is a workspace that supports the features Office Scripts rely on. This includes access to Excel on the web, cloud storage for your workbooks, and the permissions necessary to run and manage scripts. The experience is designed to be intuitive, with a dedicated Automation tab in Excel Online and a built-in editor that lets you view, write, and run scripts directly from your browser.

Setting up this environment is the first step toward modern Excel automation. It marks the beginning of a new chapter in how you approach routine tasks and complex workflows. Once you're up and running, the possibilities expand quickly—from recording simple scripts to building powerful, integrated flows that connect with other Microsoft 365 apps.

Before we go hands-on, let's take a closer look at the **requirements and tools** you'll need to get started—everything from your Microsoft 365 subscription to cloud storage options like OneDrive.

Migrating VBA Macros to Office Scripts and Power Automate

Requirements and Tools (Microsoft 365 Subscription, OneDrive, etc.)

To begin using Office Scripts, you'll need to make sure you have access to the right tools and services within the Microsoft 365 ecosystem. Unlike traditional Excel macros that operate locally, Office Scripts are designed for a cloud-based environment. This means that both your Excel files and the scripts you create will live online, enabling collaboration, automation, and integration in ways that go far beyond the desktop experience.

At the heart of this setup is a Microsoft 365 subscription that includes access to Excel for the web. Not every plan supports Office Scripts, so it's important to verify that your license—whether personal, business, or enterprise—has this functionality enabled. In most business and education plans, the feature is included by default, especially when paired with access to OneDrive or SharePoint for file storage. These cloud storage services are essential, as Office Scripts require files to be stored online in order to run. Without that connection, the automation simply can't function as intended.

In addition to the right subscription and storage, having a modern web browser and a stable internet connection will ensure a smooth experience when working with scripts in Excel Online. No installation is needed; everything runs within your browser, keeping the process lightweight and accessible. If your organization uses Microsoft 365, it's also a good idea to check with your IT administrator to confirm that Office Scripts and Power Automate are enabled for your account. Once everything is in place, you'll have the full power of script-based automation at your fingertips.

With the right tools ready, the next step is to activate and access the Office Scripts feature in your Excel Online environment. In the next section, we'll walk through the process of **enabling Office Scripts step by step**, so you can begin writing and running your first cloud-based scripts.

Enabling Office Scripts in Excel Online (Step-by-Step)

Once you've confirmed that your Microsoft 365 setup supports Office Scripts, the next step is to enable the feature within Excel Online. Fortunately, this process is straightforward and doesn't require any installations or technical configuration. Office Scripts is a built-in feature in Excel for the web, and in most cases, it's ready to use as soon as you open a workbook stored in OneDrive or SharePoint. The key is knowing where to find it—and understanding how to activate it if it isn't visible right away.

When you open a compatible Excel file in your browser, you'll typically see a tab labeled "Automate" on the ribbon at the top of the screen. This is your gateway to Office Scripts. From here, you can access recorded scripts, create new ones, and connect your workbooks to broader workflows using Power Automate. If the Automate tab isn't visible, your Microsoft 365 administrator may need to enable the feature in the admin center, particularly in managed business or enterprise environments where certain tools are restricted by policy.

Once enabled, the interface is intuitive and welcoming, even if you've never written a line of code before. You'll have access to both a script recorder and a code editor, which gives you the flexibility to start small and grow your automation skills over time. Whether you're recording your first script or writing one from scratch, Excel Online provides a clear path forward.

With Office Scripts now activated and ready to use, it's time to explore the tools you'll be working with. In the next section, we'll take a closer look at **the Excel Online Automation tab and the built-in code editor**, so you can become familiar with the layout and start building scripts with confidence.

Exploring the Excel Online Automation Tab and Code Editor

With Office Scripts enabled in Excel Online, a new world of automation becomes available through the Automation tab. This tab is where all script-related activity takes place, and it's designed to be simple and intuitive, even for users who are just beginning to explore scripting. At a glance, you'll see options to record actions, edit existing scripts, and create new ones from scratch. Everything is neatly organized, allowing you to focus on building solutions without needing to dig through menus or settings.

One of the most accessible features is the Action Recorder. This tool allows you to perform tasks in your workbook while Excel automatically captures those actions and translates them into a script. It's an ideal starting point for beginners, as it requires no coding at all. You can clean data, apply formatting, or insert formulas, and Excel will generate the corresponding script in the background. Once recorded, you can view and modify the script to better understand how the code works—and even enhance it with more advanced logic.

For those ready to dive deeper, the built-in code editor is the perfect companion. It opens in a side panel and offers a clean, distraction-free environment to write and edit scripts using TypeScript, a language similar to JavaScript. The editor includes helpful features like syntax highlighting, autocomplete, and error checking, making it easier to write correct and readable code. Whether you're customizing a recorded script or building a new one entirely by hand, the editor gives you full control over your automation logic.

Exploring the Automation tab and getting comfortable with the code editor is a key step in becoming confident with Office Scripts. Once you've familiarized yourself with these tools, you're ready to put them into action. In the next section, we'll walk through how to **record and run your very first Office Script**, helping you experience just how powerful and approachable this new way of automating Excel can be.

First Script: Recording and Running a Simple Office Script

There's something exciting about automating your first task in Excel using Office Scripts. It's that moment when you realize that repetitive, manual steps you've done countless times can now be captured, repeated, and shared—with just a few clicks. The best way to get started is by recording a simple script. This approach requires no prior coding knowledge and lets you ease into the process while watching Excel do the heavy lifting for you.

When you click on the "Record Actions" button in the Automation tab, Excel starts tracking your activity in real time. As you make changes to a workbook—like entering data, formatting cells, or sorting columns—those steps are translated into script code behind the scenes. It's a live, visual way to build your first Office Script. When you stop recording, your script is saved and ready to be played back.

You can rerun it at any time, instantly applying the same set of actions to any compatible workbook.

What makes this even more powerful is that you're not limited to just recording. Once the script is created, you can open it in the code editor to explore and even edit the code. This is where the learning truly begins. You'll start to recognize patterns, see how Excel's objects and methods are used, and gradually become more comfortable reading and writing TypeScript code. The more you experiment, the more confident you'll become in building scripts from scratch—or refining recorded ones to better suit your needs.

Running your first script is a simple yet empowering step toward modern Excel automation. It sets the stage for deeper learning and opens the door to more advanced customizations. Now that you've recorded and executed your first Office Script, you're ready to understand the language that powers it. In the next chapter, we'll explore a **TypeScript primer for Excel developers**—a practical guide for those coming from a VBA background who want to get comfortable with JavaScript and TypeScript basics.

4. TypeScript Primer for Excel Developers

If you've worked with VBA in Excel, you already understand the power of code to transform repetitive tasks into smart, automated solutions. With Office Scripts, that same potential exists—but now it's powered by TypeScript, a modern programming language that offers greater flexibility, readability, and scalability. For many Excel users, learning TypeScript might feel like stepping into a new world. But in truth, it's not as distant from VBA as it might first appear. In fact, many of the core concepts—like variables, loops, functions, and object references—are quite similar, just expressed a little differently.

TypeScript is essentially JavaScript with added structure. It helps catch errors early, provides better guidance through autocomplete and hints, and creates a more maintainable codebase—especially as scripts become more complex. For Excel automation, this means cleaner code, fewer bugs, and greater potential to integrate with modern services like Power Automate and Microsoft Graph. You don't need to become a full-fledged web developer to use it effectively. With just a basic understanding of its syntax and structure, you'll be able to write scripts that are just as powerful—and often more flexible—than traditional VBA.

Think of this primer as your bridge between the old and the new. It's designed to help you translate what you already know into a modern language that's optimized for the cloud. You'll see how your familiarity with Excel's object model and VBA logic can guide your transition to scripting with TypeScript. And as you begin to see the parallels and patterns, you'll find that learning TypeScript is less about starting from scratch and more about evolving your skill set.

To get started, let's take a closer look at the **JavaScript and TypeScript basics**—focusing specifically on what VBA users need to know about syntax and structure.

JavaScript/TypeScript Basics for VBA Users (Syntax and Structure)

For Excel users familiar with VBA, stepping into the world of JavaScript and TypeScript can initially feel unfamiliar—but it doesn't take long to find your footing. While the syntax may look different at first glance, many of the underlying principles are remarkably similar. Both VBA and TypeScript are imperative languages, which means they follow a logical, step-by-step structure. Once you get used to a few new symbols and conventions, the process of writing scripts begins to feel surprisingly intuitive.

In TypeScript, code is written using curly braces to define blocks and semicolons to end statements, which differs from the more natural-language style of VBA. Variables are declared using keywords like let or const rather than Dim, and functions are structured using parentheses and braces instead of the Sub and End Sub structure you're used to. These changes are mostly cosmetic, and once you start experimenting with simple examples, the logic becomes easy to follow.

TypeScript also brings with it the benefits of a modern development language. It's more structured than plain JavaScript, offering type checking and error highlighting that can help you avoid common mistakes before the script ever runs. This is particularly helpful for those transitioning from VBA, as it provides real-time feedback and suggestions while you write your code—similar to what the VBA editor offers, but often more advanced and supportive.

27

More importantly, learning TypeScript in the context of Office Scripts doesn't require mastering the entire language. You'll only need a focused set of concepts that apply to Excel automation. With a solid grasp of basic syntax, function structure, and how variables are handled, you'll be ready to start building effective scripts.

In the next section, we'll take a deeper dive into those key building blocks—**variables, loops, and functions**—and see how they compare between VBA and TypeScript. This comparison will help solidify your understanding and make your transition to Office Scripts even smoother.

Variables, Loops, and Functions: VBA vs. TypeScript

When moving from VBA to TypeScript, one of the most reassuring discoveries is that the core programming concepts you already know—like variables, loops, and functions—are still the foundation of everything you'll do. The logic you've used to automate Excel tasks in VBA translates naturally into TypeScript, even if the syntax looks a little different at first glance.

In VBA, declaring a variable with Dim and setting its type is second nature. In TypeScript, the approach is similar but modernized. You'll use keywords like let or const to declare variables, and although you can define types explicitly, TypeScript often detects the type automatically based on the value assigned. This flexibility makes scripting faster while still maintaining clarity and structure.

Loops are another area where your existing knowledge carries over. The classic For...Next and Do While loops in VBA have their equivalents in TypeScript, though the structure uses parentheses and braces. Whether you're iterating through rows in a worksheet or processing elements in an array, the flow of logic remains the same. And because TypeScript supports powerful loop types—such as forEach and for...of—you'll often find even cleaner ways to handle repetition than you might in VBA.

Functions in TypeScript also mirror the structure of what you've seen in VBA. Instead of using Sub or Function, you define a function using the function keyword. You can pass parameters, return values, and organize your code into reusable blocks just as you would in VBA. The difference is in the formatting, not the logic. In fact, many Excel developers find that functions in TypeScript feel even more flexible, especially when combined with the power of objects and structured data.

As you become more familiar with writing scripts in TypeScript, you'll start to see how these concepts work together to create clean, powerful automation. And to truly harness that power, it's essential to understand how Excel's structure—its workbooks, worksheets, and ranges—is represented in code. In the next section, we'll explore **Understanding Objects in TypeScript**, and see how Excel's familiar elements translate into a modern scripting environment.

Understanding Objects in TypeScript (Workbook, Worksheet, Range, etc.)

At the heart of both VBA and Office Scripts lies the Excel object model—the structured way that we interact with the contents of a workbook through code. If you've worked with VBA before, you're already familiar with objects like Workbook, Worksheet, and Range. In TypeScript, these same elements still play a central role, but they're accessed using a modern syntax and often within a more structured, asynchronous environment.

In Office Scripts, your interaction with Excel begins through a function that takes a workbook object as its entry point. From there, everything flows in a logical, hierarchical way. You use the workbook object to access individual worksheets, and from those worksheets, you target specific ranges, tables, or cells. This mirrors the approach you may have used in VBA, but with clearer structure and stricter typing, which helps prevent common mistakes and improves readability.

One noticeable difference is the way methods and properties are used. TypeScript relies on a dot notation that will feel familiar, but some names and behaviours may differ slightly. For example, while VBA allows for certain shortcuts and implicit references, TypeScript encourages clarity. You'll often need to explicitly define what you're accessing, which might take a little more typing at first—but the trade-off is greater reliability and more maintainable code in the long run.

As you write more scripts, you'll come to appreciate how the object model in Office Scripts balances familiarity with precision. You'll navigate through workbooks, select worksheets by name or index, define ranges by cell reference, and apply formatting or data transformations—all using clean, readable code. Understanding these core objects is essential to building meaningful automation that interacts with your spreadsheets exactly as you intend.

Now that you have a sense of how Excel's structure is represented in TypeScript, it's time to learn how to catch errors, track progress, and understand what's happening behind the scenes. In the next section, we'll dive into **Debugging and Logging in Office Scripts**, giving you the tools to troubleshoot issues and refine your scripts with confidence.

Debugging and Logging in Office Scripts

Even the most experienced developers make mistakes— and in scripting, debugging is a natural part of the process. When writing Office Scripts, it's important to have tools and strategies for identifying what's going wrong and understanding why a script may not behave as expected. Fortunately, Office Scripts provides simple but effective ways to observe what your code is doing, so you can troubleshoot issues with clarity and confidence.

One of the most helpful tools available is the console.log() function. This works like a virtual notebook where you can leave yourself clues during execution. By logging values at different stages of your script—like the contents of a range or the result of a calculation—you get immediate insight into how your code is behaving. These log messages appear in the Script Details pane after the script finishes running, making it easy to follow the logic and catch where things might have gone off track.

Unlike VBA, which often relies on breakpoints and step-through debugging in the editor, Office Scripts is more about writing clean, transparent code and observing its behaviour through output. Because scripts run in a secure, cloud-based environment, real-time debugging is limited—but thoughtful use of logging, careful inspection of variables, and testing in small steps can go a long way toward building stable, reliable automation.

As you become more familiar with debugging in Office Scripts, you'll start to adopt a mindset of testing as you write. Instead of waiting for errors to appear, you'll proactively include checkpoints and validations to guide development. It's a habit that not only speeds up troubleshooting but also results in scripts that are easier to maintain and share with others.

With your debugging and logging skills in place, you're ready to dive deeper into what the Office Scripts platform truly offers. In the next chapter, we'll explore an **Office Scripts API Deep Dive**, where you'll learn how to navigate the object model, work with ranges, manage tables and charts, and handle exceptions—giving you the full power of automation at your fingertips.

5. Office Scripts API Deep Dive

Once you've become familiar with the basics of TypeScript and the overall structure of Office Scripts, it's time to dive into the core of what makes this platform truly powerful: the Office Scripts API. This collection of objects, methods, and properties forms the bridge between your code and Excel's functionality. It allows you to perform everything from simple edits to complex, multi-step data transformations—all through structured, predictable code.

The API is designed to reflect the way people naturally think about Excel. You interact with workbooks, worksheets, ranges, tables, and charts using intuitive commands that mirror the steps you might take manually. Whether you're adjusting cell values, applying formatting, or generating visualizations, the API provides the tools to automate these actions with precision and control. And because it's based on a modern scripting language, your code is often shorter, clearer, and easier to maintain than its VBA equivalent.

As you deepen your understanding of the API, you'll also begin to see just how scalable your scripts can become. With support for looping through data, dynamically identifying objects, and chaining actions together, your automations can grow from simple helpers into robust, reusable tools. It's this flexibility that makes Office Scripts such an exciting option for Excel users who want to stay ahead of the curve.

Before you can fully unlock the API's potential, it's important to understand how to navigate its structure. In the next section, we'll compare how the **Office Scripts object model differs from VBA's object model**, and look at how your existing knowledge can be applied to this more modern, cloud-based environment.

Navigating the Office Scripts Object Model vs. VBA Object Model

For anyone coming from a VBA background, understanding the Office Scripts object model is both reassuring and refreshing. At its core, it follows the same logical hierarchy: workbooks contain worksheets, worksheets contain ranges, and ranges hold data. This familiar structure means you won't be starting from scratch—instead, you'll be translating your knowledge into a new, more structured and cloud-friendly language.

In VBA, you often have a great deal of flexibility—and sometimes ambiguity—when referencing objects. Excel might let you skip declaring a workbook or assume the active worksheet, which can be convenient but risky. In Office Scripts, the object model encourages explicit references. You start from a defined workbook object, and from there, you drill down to specific worksheets, tables, ranges, and other elements. This makes your code easier to follow and much less prone to unexpected behavior, especially when scripts are reused or shared with others.

One major difference you'll notice is that Office Scripts are designed to run in a stateless, cloud-based environment. This means you don't work with the "active cell" or "selection" in the same way as you might in VBA. Instead, you reference exactly what you want to manipulate, making your scripts more predictable and consistent. It's a shift in mindset—from controlling a visible interface to working with well-defined data structures—but one that quickly becomes second nature.

As you explore this object model more deeply, you'll start to appreciate its clarity and structure. It might feel a bit more formal at first, but that precision becomes incredibly valuable as your scripts grow in complexity and impact. With that foundation in place, you're now ready to get hands-on with one of the most common tasks in Excel automation. In the next section, we'll explore how to work with **ranges and cells**—including reading, writing, and applying formulas using Office Scripts.

Working with Ranges and Cells (Reading, Writing, Formulas)

Interacting with ranges and cells is at the heart of any Excel automation, and Office Scripts makes this process both powerful and approachable. Whether you're retrieving data from a column, updating specific cells, or applying formulas, the Office Scripts API gives you precise control over your spreadsheet content. And while the syntax may be different from VBA, the logic behind it will feel familiar to anyone who's worked with Excel macros in the past.

In Office Scripts, working with a range begins by referencing the worksheet and then calling a method to get a specific range, often using its address in A1 notation. Once you've identified the range, you can read its values into a variable, write new data, or assign formulas using clearly defined methods. This makes your scripts easy to understand and maintain, especially when you're manipulating large data sets or applying dynamic changes.

Reading and writing values is done with the getValues and setValues methods, which work with arrays that represent the layout of the spreadsheet. This structured approach allows for bulk operations, improving performance and efficiency. Similarly, applying formulas uses a setFormulas method, allowing you to programmatically insert calculations just as you would in a worksheet. The beauty of this setup is that it's both precise and scalable—you can update one cell or an entire range with just a few lines of code.

Formulas in Office Scripts behave as they do in Excel. You can use all the same functions, reference cells, and build complex expressions. The main difference is that you're building the logic in code, which means you can generate formulas dynamically, based on data, conditions, or inputs from other parts of your script. This opens up powerful possibilities for automation and intelligent workbook design.

With these tools at your fingertips, you can start to automate much of what once required manual input or repetitive formulas. And while working with individual cells and ranges is useful, Office Scripts becomes even more powerful when dealing with structured data. In the next section, we'll explore how to **manage tables and PivotTables**—two of Excel's most essential features for organizing and analysing data.

Managing Tables and PivotTables in Office Scripts

Tables and PivotTables are among Excel's most powerful tools for organizing and analyzing data. In Office Scripts, they become even more dynamic, giving you the ability to manipulate structured data programmatically and consistently across workbooks and teams. With a few lines of script, you can create tables, filter data, refresh PivotTables, or generate entire summaries—all without touching a single cell manually.

Working with tables in Office Scripts feels intuitive. Once you've identified the worksheet you're working with, you can easily access existing tables by name or even create new ones from a defined range. From there, you can add rows, update values, sort columns, and apply filters. Because tables are structured and self-contained, they're ideal for automation—especially when you're working with regularly updated data sources or building reusable templates.

PivotTables offer another layer of sophistication. While they have traditionally required manual setup in the interface, Office Scripts now allows you to automate their creation and refresh process. You can define the data source, choose which fields to place in rows, columns, and values, and apply formatting to produce clean, professional reports. This level of control is invaluable for workflows that rely on consistency and accuracy, especially when generating recurring reports across departments or clients.

By integrating tables and PivotTables into your Office Scripts, you're not just automating data entry—you're building intelligent systems that respond to changing information. You can design scripts that clean raw input, format it as a table, summarize it with a PivotTable, and send the final report—all in a single, repeatable flow.

Once you've mastered these data structures, the next step is visualizing the results. In the following section, we'll take a closer look at **chart automation and visualization differences** in Office Scripts, exploring how to programmatically create and customize charts to bring your data to life.

Chart Automation and Visualization Differences

Data becomes most impactful when it's easy to interpret—and charts have always played a vital role in turning raw numbers into clear, visual insights. In VBA, chart automation is possible but often requires navigating a complex and sometimes inconsistent object model. With Office Scripts,

Modern Excel Automation:

Migrating VBA Macros to Office Scripts and Power Automate

Microsoft has taken a more streamlined and modern approach, making it easier to create, modify, and style charts in a way that's both programmatic and intuitive.

Creating a chart in Office Scripts begins with identifying the data you want to visualize, typically from a range or a table. From there, you can define the chart type—such as column, line, or pie—and customize its appearance with labels, titles, and layout options. The API provides a well-structured and readable way to control the chart's behavior, making your scripts easier to write and maintain. Whether you're generating reports or building dashboards, you can include charts that update automatically based on the latest data— no manual tweaks required.

One of the key advantages of using Office Scripts for chart automation is consistency. You can standardize how charts look and behave across multiple workbooks or projects, ensuring that your presentations and reports always follow the same visual language. This not only saves time but also enhances professionalism and clarity.

While Office Scripts currently support many of the essential chart types and customization options, it's worth noting that some advanced features available in desktop Excel may not yet be fully mirrored in the online version. However, Microsoft is continually expanding the capabilities of the Excel Online charting engine, so we can expect ongoing improvements in flexibility and visual power.

Of course, as with any code, things don't always go perfectly on the first run. That's why it's important to understand how to detect and handle problems gracefully. In the next section, we'll cover **handling errors and exceptions in scripts**, giving you the tools to write more robust and reliable automations.

Handling Errors and Exceptions in Scripts

No matter how carefully a script is written, errors are an inevitable part of automation. Whether it's due to a missing worksheet, unexpected data format, or simply a typo in a range reference, things can go wrong. What matters most is how your script responds when it happens. Office Scripts provides mechanisms for detecting and managing errors in a way that keeps your automation running smoothly and protects your users from confusion or data loss.

Unlike VBA, which often uses On Error Resume Next or On Error GoTo constructs, Office Scripts leverages the try...catch structure common in JavaScript and TypeScript. This method allows you to clearly separate the logic that might fail from the response when it does. It helps you write scripts that not only handle failures gracefully but also provide meaningful feedback. For example, if a script is supposed to update a specific worksheet that doesn't exist, you can catch the error, log it, or even notify the user—rather than letting the script crash silently or stop without explanation.

Proper error handling also makes it easier to troubleshoot and maintain your scripts over time. When a script fails, detailed error messages or custom logs can tell you exactly where the problem occurred and why. This transparency is especially useful in shared environments where multiple users rely on the same automation. Adding thoughtful logging and fallback behavior can make the difference between a brittle, frustrating macro and a dependable, professional-grade solution.

As you build more advanced automations, incorporating error and exception handling into your workflow will become second nature. It's part of writing robust, production-ready scripts—especially when you begin replacing older VBA processes with modern alternatives.

And that brings us to the next important step: **migration**. In the following chapter, we'll explore **Migration Strategies and Best Practices**, where you'll learn how to plan, refactor, and validate your VBA macros as you transition them into scalable, cloud-based Office Scripts.

6. Migration Strategies and Best Practices

Migrating from VBA to Office Scripts isn't just about rewriting code—it's about rethinking how automation fits into a modern, cloud-first environment. As organizations move away from legacy desktop workflows toward more collaborative and secure solutions, the shift to Office Scripts represents both a technical upgrade and a strategic opportunity. But like any transition, it requires thoughtful planning, clear goals, and a structured approach to ensure the new solutions are not only functional, but future-proof.

One of the key advantages of Office Scripts is its compatibility with the broader Microsoft 365 ecosystem. Instead of working in isolation, your scripts can become part of larger workflows that span across Teams, SharePoint, Outlook, and beyond. This opens up exciting possibilities for automation—but also means that successful migration demands more than just a line-by-line conversion. It's important to understand the intent behind each macro, evaluate its dependencies, and reimagine it in a way that aligns with cloud-based logic and user experience.

Best practices come into play throughout the migration process. From breaking down large macros into smaller, reusable scripts, to adding clear comments and consistent naming conventions, these small habits contribute to more maintainable and readable code. Error handling, performance optimization, and version control all take on new importance when your scripts are running in shared or automated environments.

The most successful migrations are those that focus not just on replicating functionality, but on improving it. In many cases, Office Scripts can deliver faster execution, better error management, and cleaner code—especially when combined with tools like Power Automate for orchestrating tasks across services.

To make that kind of transformation possible, you'll need a well-structured migration plan. In the next section, we'll explore how to **plan a VBA to Office Scripts migration project**, laying the foundation for a smooth, efficient, and rewarding transition.

Planning a VBA to Office Scripts Migration Project

Every successful migration begins with a clear plan. Transitioning from VBA to Office Scripts is not just a technical exercise—it's a strategic process that involves understanding your existing workflows, identifying opportunities for improvement, and designing solutions that are sustainable in a modern, cloud-based environment. Taking the time to plan your migration carefully can help prevent disruption, reduce rework, and ultimately deliver better results.

The first step in any migration project is understanding what needs to be migrated—and why. This means taking a close look at the macros currently in use, identifying which ones are business-critical, which are outdated or redundant, and which could benefit from modernization. It also means thinking about how users interact with those macros. Are they tied to desktop-only workflows? Do they depend on local files or user input? Are they run on a schedule, or triggered by specific events? These questions help define the scope of your project and shape the approach you'll take.

Once you have a clear picture of your starting point, it becomes easier to prioritize. Some macros may be simple and easy to convert, while others may require significant restructuring to fit into the Office Scripts model. Creating a roadmap with phases or milestones can help you manage the migration process incrementally, testing and refining as you go. Collaboration with users, stakeholders, and IT teams ensures that the new scripts meet expectations and align with broader goals like security, accessibility, and integration.

Planning also includes allocating time for training and documentation. Since Office Scripts uses TypeScript and integrates with tools like Power Automate, there may be a learning curve for teams used to VBA. Investing in skill-building up front helps build confidence and reduces support requests down the line. Ultimately, a well-planned migration project isn't just about transferring functionality—it's about laying the groundwork for smarter, more connected automation across your organization.

With the plan in place, the next step is to take a closer look at what you're migrating. In the following section, we'll explore **analyzing legacy macros**—including how to assess their complexity, dependencies, and overall compatibility with the Office Scripts environment.

Analyzing Legacy Macros (Complexity, Dependencies, Compatibility)

Before diving into rewriting code, it's essential to take a step back and fully understand what your existing VBA macros are doing. Legacy macros often evolve over time, with layers of logic added to meet changing needs. As a result, they may contain hidden complexity, undocumented dependencies, and tight coupling to the desktop environment. Analyzing these scripts carefully will help you avoid surprises later and allow for smarter, more focused migration work.

A good analysis begins with looking at how each macro fits into the bigger picture. Some scripts are simple and self-contained, performing repetitive formatting or data entry tasks. Others might span multiple worksheets, rely on user inputs, or connect to external files and applications. Recognizing these levels of complexity early allows you to break the migration into manageable parts and decide where to focus your efforts. It also helps you determine whether a macro should be migrated as-is, redesigned for better performance, or even retired if it's no longer relevant.

Dependencies play a crucial role in this process. Many VBA macros rely on specific workbook structures, local file paths, or external add-ins that may not be available—or even possible—in a cloud environment. Identifying these dependencies up front gives you time to design workarounds or update processes so they work with cloud-native tools like OneDrive or SharePoint. Compatibility is another key consideration. Not all VBA functions have direct equivalents in Office Scripts, so it's important to flag any features that may need alternative solutions or rethinking.

The more insight you gather during this analysis, the smoother your transition will be. You'll be able to plan your refactoring work more effectively, anticipate user needs, and build scripts that are both functional and maintainable in the long run. The goal isn't to translate VBA line by line, but to preserve the core functionality while embracing the strengths of the modern scripting environment.

With this understanding in place, the next step is to begin reworking your code for the cloud. In the following section, we'll look at how to **refactor VBA logic for Office Scripts**, including how to handle state, user inputs, and other key differences between desktop and web-based automation.

Refactoring VBA Logic for the Cloud (State, User Inputs, etc.)

Refactoring legacy VBA code for use in Office Scripts is more than just translating syntax—it's about rethinking how your logic fits into a new, cloud-based model. Many VBA scripts were written in a world where workbooks ran on a single user's desktop, with the ability to interact directly with the screen, respond to mouse clicks, and pause for user inputs. Office Scripts, by contrast, are designed for web-based, stateless execution, often as part of broader workflows involving automation tools like Power Automate.

One of the first challenges you may encounter is managing state. In VBA, you can store values in global variables or rely on selections made in the interface. Office Scripts, however, operate without persistent state or access to the user's active selection. This requires a more explicit approach— where every variable is passed, returned, or stored in defined cells or ranges. It encourages clarity and modularity, which ultimately leads to more maintainable code. You'll begin to write scripts that clearly define where data comes from and where it's going, with no reliance on what the user might have selected.

User input is another area where refactoring becomes necessary. VBA scripts often use input boxes or message boxes to gather information. Office Scripts don't include these interactive prompts, especially when run as part of automated flows. Instead, inputs are often passed in programmatically through parameters or triggered by external events, like changes in a file or a submission from a form. This change in design pattern shifts your thinking from reactive, interface-driven automation to proactive, data-driven scripting.

As you refactor, it helps to focus on the core purpose of your original macros. What problem were they solving? What business logic did they automate? Once you've clarified that, it becomes easier to reshape the code into functions that are compatible with the web—leaner, clearer, and often more efficient than the original.

Refactoring is where your migration really begins to take shape. You're not just rewriting—you're rebuilding smarter, more future-ready automation. And to keep things maintainable, readable, and easy to scale, it's essential to follow sound development habits. In the next section, we'll explore the **best practices for writing efficient and readable Office Scripts**, helping you build clean code that others can understand and reuse with confidence.

Best Practices for Efficient, Readable Office Scripts

Writing code that works is one thing—writing code that's clear, efficient, and easy to maintain is another. As you move from VBA to Office Scripts, adopting best practices from the start will help you build automation that not only performs well but also stands the test of time. Whether you're creating scripts for your own use or developing solutions that others will depend on, clean code is a powerful asset.

One of the key principles of good scripting in Office Scripts is clarity. Since these scripts are often used in collaborative, cloud-based environments, it's important that others can understand your logic without needing to decipher cryptic variable names or unravel nested functions. Using descriptive names, adding helpful comments, and organizing your code into logical sections all contribute to scripts that are easier to read, review, and reuse. Even small things—like consistent formatting and indentation—make a big difference when someone else has to step in and make changes later on.

Efficiency is equally important. Office Scripts interact with Excel's workbook objects in a structured way, and minimizing unnecessary calls to those objects can significantly improve performance. For example, reading or writing large blocks of data at once is far faster than looping through individual cells. By planning how your script accesses data, you can avoid slowdowns and make sure your automation runs smoothly—even with large datasets.

Another best practice is modular thinking. Instead of writing one long script that tries to do everything, break your code into smaller, reusable pieces. This makes it easier to test, debug, and update individual parts without affecting the whole. It also makes your scripts more flexible—you can adapt or reuse specific functions in future projects with minimal effort.

Ultimately, readable and efficient scripts are about more than just style. They reflect a thoughtful approach to automation—one that respects both the complexity of Excel and the need for maintainable, scalable solutions. By following these practices, you'll not only make your scripts better but also more valuable to your team or organization.

Once your scripts are in place, the final step is making sure they work as intended. In the next section, we'll explore how to **test and validate your new Office Scripts** against the original VBA macros, ensuring a smooth and reliable transition from old to new.

Testing and Validating the New Scripts vs. Old Macros

Once you've completed the migration of a macro from VBA to Office Scripts, the next critical step is ensuring that the new script performs as expected. Testing is where your planning, refactoring, and development work come together. It's not just about verifying functionality—it's about building confidence that the new script is reliable, accurate, and ready for everyday use. After all, replacing a well-established VBA macro means delivering the same results with improved efficiency and scalability.

Validation starts by comparing outputs. If your original macro produced a report, formatted a worksheet, or processed data in a specific way, your Office Script should produce identical or improved results. Running both versions side by side using the same input allows you to spot differences and refine the logic where needed. This isn't always a one-to-one comparison—Office Scripts may introduce enhancements or streamline certain steps—but the overall outcome should remain consistent.

It's also important to simulate real-world usage. Testing in controlled conditions is helpful, but scripts often behave differently when interacting with larger datasets, shared workbooks, or automated workflows. Pay attention to edge cases, such as empty cells, missing sheets, or unexpected user inputs. Incorporating error-handling and logging into your Office Script will not only help identify issues during testing but will also make the script more robust when deployed.

Don't overlook the value of user feedback during validation. If others rely on the macro you're replacing, involve them in testing the new script. Their insights can highlight subtle expectations or usage habits that aren't obvious in the code but matter a great deal in practice. A script that feels familiar and intuitive will be more readily adopted, even if it's built with entirely new tools behind the scenes.

Once your Office Script has passed validation and proven its reliability, it's ready to take over. You've not only completed a technical migration—you've delivered a more modern, maintainable solution that supports the future of Excel automation.

To see these concepts in action, the next chapter walks through a **hands-on migration case study**, where we'll take a real-world reporting workflow and show how to reimagine it using Office Scripts—from scenario setup and VBA analysis to a full rewrite and result verification.

7. Hands-On Migration Case Study: Part 1 – *Automating a Reporting Workflow*

Theory and best practices are essential when learning a new tool, but the true test comes when you apply that knowledge to a real-world scenario. In this chapter, we step away from abstract concepts and walk through a complete, hands-on migration—from an existing VBA macro to a fully functional Office Script. This case study is designed to bring everything you've learned so far to life, showing you how the process unfolds from start to finish in a practical, relatable way.

The focus here is on a typical reporting workflow—something many Excel users automate to save time and ensure consistency. It's the kind of macro that runs weekly or monthly, pulling data together, formatting it, maybe adding charts or summaries, and saving the results for distribution. These macros often evolve over years, growing in complexity and becoming deeply embedded in business routines. That makes them ideal candidates for migration—not just to modernize the code, but to unlock new potential with cloud-based tools and integrations.

As we guide you through this project, you'll see how to analyze the original VBA logic, identify inefficiencies or limitations, and redesign the automation using Office Scripts. You'll follow the thinking behind the changes, compare the code side by side, and test the result to make sure it meets all the original requirements—if not improves upon them.

This case study is meant to be practical, hands-on, and repeatable. You'll come away with a clear understanding of the migration journey, as well as a blueprint you can adapt to your own projects.

To begin, let's take a look at the **scenario overview**, where we'll compare the legacy VBA macro with the modern solution we're about to build.

Scenario Overview: Legacy VBA Macro vs. Modern Solution

Let's imagine a common business scenario: each week, a team receives updated raw sales data. This data needs to be cleaned, sorted, formatted into a report, and saved as a finalized file for distribution. In many organizations, a VBA macro has long been responsible for this task—automating the process of copying data, applying filters, adding totals, formatting headers, and saving the file to a local drive. It's a solution that works, but one that's tightly tied to the desktop version of Excel, dependent on a specific user environment, and often fragile when something changes.

As workflows evolve and companies move to cloud-first environments, these kinds of macros begin to show their age. The need for cross-device compatibility, real-time collaboration, and integration with platforms like SharePoint or Teams makes desktop-bound automation feel limiting. That's where Office Scripts comes in—offering a modern, cloud-based way to reimagine these same workflows using Excel Online and Power Automate. Instead of running manually on one user's computer, the new script can run from anywhere, automatically, and even be triggered by events or schedules.

In this case study, we'll compare the legacy VBA macro with a streamlined Office Script that performs the same reporting task. Along the way, we'll highlight not only the differences in code structure but also in mindset—moving from a static, file-based routine to a more dynamic, flexible process that's built for scale and collaboration.

To begin our transformation, we'll first break down the existing VBA solution. In the next section, we'll walk through the **Original VBA Macro**, examining what it does, where it works well, and where the pain points begin to show

Original VBA Macro Walkthrough (What it Does, Pain Points)

The legacy VBA macro at the centre of this case study was designed to streamline the weekly reporting process. Its purpose was simple but essential: take a raw data export—typically pasted into the first worksheet of an Excel file—and transform it into a polished, presentation-ready report. This included sorting the data, applying filters, calculating totals, formatting headers, and saving the result as a separate file for sharing. The macro was triggered manually, often by a team member clicking a button or using a keyboard shortcut.

In practice, this macro performed its function reliably for years. It saved the team time, ensured consistency, and reduced the risk of human error. However, over time, its limitations became increasingly apparent. It relied heavily on fixed references, assuming that data would always start in the same cell and follow the same structure. Any change in the layout of the raw export—even a new column or an unexpected blank row—could cause the macro to break. Additionally, because it ran on a local machine, only one person could execute it, and it required access to local file paths that weren't compatible with a cloud-based workflow.

Another challenge was maintenance. The macro had grown over time, with patches and fixes added to address edge cases. It wasn't always easy to read or modify, especially for users unfamiliar with VBA. As the organization moved to Microsoft 365, the limitations of this desktop-bound automation became harder to overlook. Team members began requesting a solution that could run in the cloud, integrate with SharePoint, and ideally operate with little to no manual involvement.

This creates the perfect opportunity to rethink the solution using Office Scripts. In the next section, we'll explore **Designing the Office Script Replacement**, including the overall approach, key considerations, and a high-level look at how the new automation will be structured through pseudocode.

Designing the Office Script Replacement (Approach and Pseudocode)

Designing a modern replacement for a legacy VBA macro isn't just about copying functionality—it's about reimagining the process through the lens of flexibility, scalability, and maintainability. With Office Scripts, the goal is to create a cloud-based solution that's just as effective as the original macro, but better aligned with how people work in the Microsoft 365 ecosystem. Before jumping into code, it's essential to take a step back and think through the logic, flow, and structure of the script you're about to write.

The original macro we're replacing was procedural and linear, performing one task after another in a fixed order. That same structure can be preserved in Office Scripts, but with clearer modular separation and reusable functions. We begin by outlining each step: accessing the source worksheet, identifying the data range, applying filters and sorting, calculating totals, formatting headers, and finally saving or preparing the output. Each of these operations can be framed in TypeScript functions or script blocks, keeping the logic organized and readable.

Another important design consideration is how to make the script resilient and adaptable. Rather than hardcoding cell references or relying on fixed worksheet names, we'll aim to make the script dynamic—capable of identifying headers automatically, detecting the size of data ranges, and adapting to minor changes in structure. This helps future-proof the automation and reduce the risk of failure when something unexpected appears in the input data.

Pseudocode is especially useful at this stage. It allows you to map out your logic in plain language, focusing on what the script needs to do without worrying about syntax. This makes it easier to review the logic with stakeholders or teammates before diving into the actual TypeScript implementation. Once the approach is clear and agreed upon, writing the script becomes much smoother.

With our plan in place, it's time to bring the design to life. In the next section, we'll walk through a **step-by-step code rewrite**, showing the original VBA macro side by side with its Office Script equivalent—highlighting both the differences in syntax and the evolution in design.

Step-by-Step Code Rewrite (with Side-by-Side VBA and TypeScript)

Now that we have a clear design for the Office Script replacement, it's time to turn that plan into working code. To make the migration as practical and accessible as possible, we'll walk through the transformation step by step—comparing the original VBA macro to its modern TypeScript equivalent. This side-by-side approach not only shows how the syntax differs but also highlights the opportunities for cleaner, more structured automation in the cloud.

Let's start with a simple example from our reporting workflow: selecting the data range from a worksheet and applying a filter. In VBA, that might look like this:

```vba
Sub FormatReport()
    Sheets("RawData").Activate
    Range("A1").CurrentRegion.Select
    Selection.AutoFilter
End Sub
```

This macro selects the current region of data on the "RawData" sheet and applies an AutoFilter. While effective, it relies on implicit actions like activating a sheet and selecting a range—things that Office Scripts doesn't support in the same way.

Here's how we would write the same logic using Office Scripts:

```typescript
function main(workbook: ExcelScript.Workbook) {
    const sheet =
workbook.getWorksheet("RawData");
    const range =
sheet.getRange("A1").getSurroundingRegion();
    range.getAutoFilter() ??
range.getWorksheet().getAutoFilter().apply(range);
}
```

Instead of activating sheets and selecting cells, we directly reference the worksheet and define the range in a more precise, object-oriented way. This makes the script cleaner and more predictable, especially when used in shared or automated environments.

Let's expand the example to include formatting header rows. In VBA, this might look like:

```
With Range("A1:Z1")
    .Font.Bold = True
    .Interior.Color = RGB(200, 200, 255)
End With
```

The Office Scripts equivalent would be:

```
const header = sheet.getRange("A1:Z1");
header.getFormat().getFont().setBold(true);
header.getFormat().getFill().setColor("#C8C8FF"
);
```

While slightly more verbose, this approach gives greater clarity and control. The use of structured objects for formatting allows for consistent styling and easier debugging, especially in larger scripts.

By continuing this pattern, we can build out the entire report automation—from sorting and totaling to exporting or saving—while preserving the original intent of the VBA macro. The end result is a modern, readable, and reusable script that's ready to run in Excel Online, either on demand or as part of a Power Automate flow.

This step-by-step rewrite not only modernizes your workflow—it helps you rethink how automation can fit into a connected, cloud-based ecosystem.

Now that we've written and refined the script, the final step is to see it in action. In the next section, we'll walk through **running the Office Script in Excel Online and verifying results**, making sure everything works as expected and delivers the same (or better) value as the original macro.

Running the Office Script in Excel Online and Verifying Results

With the Office Script written and ready, the next step is to bring it to life inside Excel Online. Unlike VBA macros, which are run from the desktop interface with buttons or shortcuts, Office Scripts are executed directly in the browser—either manually through the Automate tab or automatically via Power Automate. This cloud-native experience removes the limitations of device dependency and makes automation more accessible across teams.

To run the script, open the workbook in Excel Online, navigate to the **Automate** tab, and select the script you created. With one click, the script will process the data just as your old VBA macro did—but now, it happens in a clean, modern environment without the need for local files, ActiveX components, or worrying whether macros are enabled. The output appears instantly, with the data sorted, headers formatted, and filters applied exactly as planned.

After running the script, validating the results is key. Start by comparing the output with what the legacy VBA macro used to generate. Look for consistency in formatting, accuracy in totals, and reliability across different datasets. For instance, if the source data changes in size from week to week, confirm that the script still identifies the correct range. You might even test it with slight variations—extra columns, missing rows, different date formats—to ensure it's resilient.

To take it one step further, you can connect this script to a Power Automate flow. For example, you could build a process where the script runs automatically when a new file is added to a SharePoint folder or when someone submits a form. This elevates the automation from a manual tool to a fully hands-free solution—modernizing not just your code, but your entire workflow.

The ability to run, validate, and schedule scripts in Excel Online is what truly sets Office Scripts apart. You're no longer limited by where or how the automation runs. Instead, you have a flexible, cloud-first engine that can adapt to your evolving needs.

With the reporting workflow complete, it's time to tackle another common use case—one that many teams struggle with: combining and cleaning data across multiple workbooks. In the next chapter, we'll explore **Part 2 of our Hands-On Migration Case Study**, where we'll look at how to consolidate spreadsheets using Office Scripts, replacing complex VBA routines with cleaner, more scalable solutions.

8. Hands-On Migration Case Study: Part 2 – *Data Processing and Cleanup*

After successfully automating a reporting workflow in the previous case study, we now shift our focus to another real-world challenge—processing and cleaning data across multiple workbooks. This is one of the most common and time-consuming tasks Excel users face, especially when dealing with regular updates, shared data sources, or department-level files that need to be combined into a single, unified dataset.

In the past, this type of task would be handled using VBA, with scripts that open workbooks one by one, copy data from predefined ranges, and paste it into a master sheet. While this approach can work, it tends to be fragile, hard to maintain, and heavily reliant on local file paths and manual file handling. It's also prone to errors if filenames change, sheets are renamed, or data structures vary slightly between files.

With Office Scripts, the approach changes dramatically. Rather than working on individual files manually, we can design a script that dynamically loops through a list of cloud-stored workbooks—such as those in a OneDrive or SharePoint folder—and pulls in the data we need with minimal effort. This automation can be triggered through Power Automate, scheduled to run regularly, or initiated by a specific event like a new file upload.

This case study is all about turning what was once a multi-step, repetitive process into a streamlined, scalable workflow. You'll see how we clean and merge datasets from

59

several workbooks into one, while handling inconsistencies and ensuring that the final output is consistent, clean, and ready for analysis. The script will identify the relevant ranges, standardize the headers, skip empty rows, and remove duplicates—tasks that would take considerable time if done manually.

This project demonstrates just how transformative Office Scripts can be—not just in replicating what VBA once did, but in rethinking how data processing should work in a cloud-first world. It's not just about saving time—it's about improving accuracy, reducing dependency on individuals, and building solutions that scale with your organization.

To begin, let's take a closer look at the **scenario overview**, where we'll explore the specifics of consolidating data across multiple workbooks and the goals for our new Office Script solution.

Scenario Overview: Consolidating Data across Workbooks

In many organizations, data is collected and stored in multiple workbooks—often one per department, region, or project. These files usually follow a similar structure but arrive separately, requiring someone to manually open each workbook, copy the relevant data, and paste it into a central master file. This routine might happen weekly, monthly, or even daily, depending on the workflow. It's repetitive, time-consuming, and highly prone to human error—especially as the number of source files grows.

Imagine a scenario where a company's regional sales managers submit their weekly reports as Excel files stored in a shared OneDrive folder. Each file contains a worksheet named "WeeklyData" with the same columns: region, salesperson, revenue, and units sold. The central office needs to combine all of these into a single workbook to produce a company-wide summary report. The old process involved manually opening each file, copying the rows, and pasting them one after another into a consolidation sheet—taking hours and introducing mistakes when files were overlooked or headers were inconsistent.

This is a perfect use case for automation with Office Scripts. By designing a script that loops through all files in a specified folder and automatically extracts the contents of the "WeeklyData" sheet from each workbook, we can eliminate the manual work entirely. The script can check for consistent headers, skip blank rows, and even remove duplicates or outdated records. This not only improves accuracy and speed but also ensures the process can run automatically—triggered by file uploads or scheduled to run at specific intervals.

With the right setup, this kind of data consolidation becomes a background task that "just works," freeing up analysts and coordinators to focus on interpreting the data rather than managing it.

In the next section, we'll take a closer look at the **challenges this process presents when using VBA**—from manual effort and maintenance headaches to the limitations of working outside the cloud.

Challenges in VBA (Maintenance, Manual Steps)

While VBA has long been the go-to tool for automating Excel tasks, its limitations become more visible when applied to repetitive, multi-file processes—like consolidating data across several workbooks. A typical VBA solution for this task involves hardcoding file paths, opening each workbook one by one, selecting ranges, and copying data into a master file. It works—until something changes. Maybe a file is renamed, the worksheet structure is slightly different, or a user adds an extra column. Suddenly, the macro throws an error, and someone has to step in and fix it.

One of the biggest challenges with VBA in this context is its dependency on a fixed environment. Scripts often rely on specific folder structures on a local drive or mapped network locations. This makes them difficult to share or scale, especially in modern organizations that increasingly use OneDrive or SharePoint. Since VBA runs on the desktop version of Excel, automation is limited to users who have the macro-enabled file open, and often, the script can't run unattended—it requires manual launching, constant monitoring, and occasional cleanup when something breaks.

Another issue is that VBA macros handling workbook consolidation tend to grow unwieldy. As more features are added—such as error-checking, logging, or formatting—the script becomes more complex and harder to maintain. Adding support for new input files might require rewriting parts of the code or inserting new case-by-case logic. Over time, these macros can become fragile, bloated, and dependent on specific users who understand their quirks.

For example, consider a VBA script that loops through 20 regional sales files every Friday morning. If one file is missing or has a different sheet name, the entire process can stop. There's no built-in resilience, no logging unless it's manually added, and no easy way to run the task remotely or on a schedule. It creates bottlenecks and requires constant attention—precisely the kind of scenario where a modern automation platform can bring major improvements.

Modern Excel Automation:

Migrating VBA Macros to Office Scripts and Power Automate

That's where Office Scripts offers a cleaner, more reliable path forward. In the next section, we'll explore how to **build a cloud-based solution using Office Scripts** that performs the same task—merging data from multiple files—but with far less manual effort, stronger stability, and full compatibility with the modern Microsoft 365 environment.

Office Scripts Solution (Using Script to Merge Data)

Replacing a complex, maintenance-heavy VBA macro with a cloud-based Office Script is more than a technical upgrade—it's a transformation in how automation works in Excel. With Office Scripts, the process of consolidating data from multiple workbooks becomes cleaner, more reliable, and fully integrated into the Microsoft 365 ecosystem. Instead of relying on a local machine to open files and copy ranges, scripts can now run directly in the cloud, triggered by events or scheduled to execute automatically through Power Automate.

Let's consider the same scenario we looked at earlier: weekly sales reports are submitted by multiple regional managers and saved in a shared OneDrive folder. The Office Script solution accesses this folder, loops through each workbook, finds the worksheet named "WeeklyData," and extracts the relevant range. It then appends this data into a master worksheet within a central report file. Because this all happens online, the user doesn't need to open any files manually—the process runs in the background, completing in a fraction of the time.

The script doesn't just collect raw data—it can also validate consistency across files. For example, if a column is missing or the header row is different, the script can log the error and skip that file, ensuring the final result isn't compromised. It can also remove duplicates, ignore blank rows, and normalize formatting across all data sources. All of this happens dynamically, with no hardcoding of file paths or assumptions about workbook names—just smart, adaptable logic that fits the cloud model.

One of the most powerful aspects of this approach is that it scales effortlessly. Adding new input files doesn't require changing the script—it just picks them up from the folder automatically. And because the output lives in SharePoint or OneDrive, it's instantly accessible to everyone who needs it, with no need to send files around or worry about version control.

This approach doesn't just replicate the VBA solution—it improves it on every front. It's more flexible, more maintainable, and far better suited to modern, distributed teams.

Now that we understand the solution's structure and capabilities, let's walk through the **code implementation step by step**, explaining how each part works and why it was designed that way.

Code Implementation with Explanations

With the strategy for data consolidation clearly outlined, it's time to translate that into working code using Office Scripts. The beauty of scripting in this environment is the balance it offers between precision and simplicity. Each part of the script serves a clear purpose, and once the logic is in place, the automation becomes repeatable, reliable, and easy to maintain—even as new files are added or data structures evolve.

Modern Excel Automation:

Migrating VBA Macros to Office Scripts and Power Automate

The script begins by defining the master workbook, which serves as the destination for all collected data. It then opens each source workbook—either through a list of file references passed in from Power Automate or by manually referencing known file URLs. From there, it locates the worksheet named "WeeklyData," dynamically identifies the data range using getUsedRange() or getRange("A1").getSurroundingRegion(), and reads the values into memory.

Here's an example of how data might be extracted from a source file:

```
let sourceSheet =
sourceWorkbook.getWorksheet("WeeklyData");
let dataRange = sourceSheet.getUsedRange();
let data = dataRange.getValues();
```

Once the script retrieves the data, it appends the rows—skipping the header if needed—into the master worksheet in the destination workbook. This is typically done using setValues() on a target range, calculating the insertion point based on the current row count:

```
let destinationSheet =
workbook.getWorksheet("MasterData");
let lastRow =
destinationSheet.getUsedRange().getRowCount();
destinationSheet.getRangeByIndexes(lastRow, 0,
data.length - 1, data[0].length)
                .setValues(data.slice(1)); //
skip header
```

Additional logic can be added to ensure the headers match, to remove duplicates, or to clean up blank rows. What's important is that every action is explicit—there's no reliance on selections, no unpredictable behavior caused by user interaction, and no guesswork about where the data ends up.

The result is a clean, efficient script that handles a task which previously required a half-hour of manual work in seconds. It's also far easier to adapt when something changes. For instance, if a new column is added to the "WeeklyData" worksheet, the script can be modified in one place—without needing to touch multiple nested loops or fragile conditionals, as might be the case in a large VBA macro.

Now that we've seen how the solution is built and why each part matters, the final step is evaluating how it performs in practice. In the next section, we'll take a look at the **before-and-after results**, comparing the performance, reliability, and maintainability of the old VBA approach versus the new Office Scripts automation.

Before-and-After Performance and Reliability

The difference between the legacy VBA approach and the Office Scripts solution becomes immediately clear once the automation is up and running. In the old process, consolidating weekly sales data from multiple workbooks could take anywhere from 20 to 40 minutes, depending on how many files were involved and whether any issues came up—like inconsistent headers, broken formulas, or missing sheets. The macro had to be run manually, often by a single team member who understood its quirks, and troubleshooting became a weekly ritual.

After implementing the Office Script version, the same process is completed in under a minute—and no one has to be present when it runs. The automation reliably collects data from all new workbooks stored in a designated OneDrive folder, appends it to a master sheet, and ensures formatting consistency across the board. Even better, it handles exceptions gracefully, logging skipped files if something unexpected occurs, rather than halting the entire process.

Another major improvement is in stability. VBA macros are known to be sensitive to user actions or environmental changes. If a user moves a file, changes a sheet name, or interrupts the macro while it's running, it can cause a crash or corrupt the output. Office Scripts, on the other hand, operate in a cloud-based environment where these factors are more controlled. There's no "active window," no reliance on selections, and no interface interruptions—just structured, dependable execution.

The benefits don't stop at speed and reliability. The new script is easier to maintain, thanks to its modular structure and cloud-based design. Updates are made in a shared environment, so changes take effect for everyone without having to email around updated macro-enabled workbooks. As new reporting requirements come in—say, adding a column for discounts or adjusting date ranges—those changes can be implemented quickly, tested instantly, and rolled out smoothly.

In short, the migration from VBA to Office Scripts doesn't just replicate the old workflow—it transforms it. It's faster, safer, and far more sustainable for a modern team working across devices and locations.

The next step is to take that automation even further by integrating it with other services using Microsoft Power Automate. In the next chapter, we'll explore how to **connect Office Scripts with Power Automate**, enabling your scripts to run on a schedule, react to triggers, and become part of full end-to-end workflows without writing a single additional line of VBA.

Modern Excel Automation:

Migrating VBA Macros to Office Scripts and Power Automate

9. Integrating Office Scripts with Power Automate

While Office Scripts can significantly modernize Excel automation on their own, their real power is fully unleashed when integrated with Power Automate. By connecting your scripts to cloud flows, you move from manual, file-by-file execution to a fully automated system that responds to triggers, schedules, and external data sources. This integration brings Excel automation into a broader digital ecosystem, allowing your workflows to span across apps like SharePoint, Outlook, Teams, and beyond.

Imagine a common scenario: every time a regional manager submits a new report to a SharePoint folder, you want that file to be processed automatically—cleaned, consolidated, and updated into a master workbook. With Power Automate, this becomes simple. You can set up a trigger to launch the Office Script as soon as a new file is detected. There's no need for someone to be present, click a button, or even open Excel. The entire process happens quietly in the background, saving time and reducing human error.

Another powerful example is scheduling. If your reporting process needs to run every Friday at 8 a.m., you can use Power Automate to execute your Office Script on a recurring schedule. No more relying on a teammate to remember to run a macro. The script will retrieve data, update reports, and notify the team when the task is complete. This makes your automation proactive, rather than reactive.

Power Automate also lets you chain multiple steps together. You can kick off a script that processes a workbook, then send a summary email via Outlook, update a SharePoint list, or store a backup copy in OneDrive. The ability to create

69

these multi-step, cross-application flows transforms Office Scripts from simple spreadsheet helpers into powerful components of business-wide automation strategies.

As your automation needs grow more sophisticated, this kind of integration allows your scripts to adapt with minimal effort. Instead of writing more code, you design smarter flows—combining the strengths of scripting and cloud orchestration.

To start taking advantage of this integration, you first need to understand the basics of working with Power Automate. In the next section, we'll walk through **Getting Started with Power Automate for Excel**, showing you how to set up your first flow, connect it to your Office Script, and begin building smart, automated processes that run on your terms.

Getting Started with Power Automate for Excel

If you've never used Power Automate before, integrating it with Excel might feel like stepping into unfamiliar territory— but the learning curve is surprisingly gentle, especially when you're starting with Office Scripts. Power Automate is a cloud-based service that lets you build flows—automated processes that connect different Microsoft 365 apps. When paired with Excel, it allows you to trigger scripts based on events, schedules, or other app activity, turning routine tasks into seamless, background workflows.

To get started, all you need is a Microsoft 365 account with access to both Excel Online and Power Automate. The easiest way to explore the integration is to open your workbook in Excel for the web and click the **Automate** tab. From there, you can create a new script or choose an existing one. Once your script is saved, you'll be able to link it to a Power Automate flow directly from within the same interface.

Imagine you have a report that needs to be refreshed every time new data is uploaded to a OneDrive folder. Instead of manually opening Excel and running your Office Script, you can create a Power Automate flow that starts with a "When a file is created" trigger. After that, you simply add an **Excel Online (Business)** action to run the Office Script on the newly uploaded file. The entire process can happen behind the scenes, with zero manual intervention.

You can also run scripts based on schedule, like generating a sales dashboard every Monday at 6 a.m. Or you might want to trigger a script after a Microsoft Form is submitted, pulling the responses into an Excel workbook and cleaning up the data. These use cases showcase how automation can remove the friction from repetitive tasks and help teams work more efficiently.

Once you've set up your first flow and seen it work in action, the possibilities quickly expand. With just a few clicks, you'll start thinking not just about what you can automate in Excel, but how your spreadsheet can be part of larger, smarter workflows across your entire organization.

In the next section, we'll take a deeper dive into **Running Office Scripts via Cloud Flows**, where we'll explore how triggers and actions work, and how to design flows that interact with your scripts in powerful and customizable ways.

Running Office Scripts via Cloud Flows (Triggers & Actions)

One of the most powerful features of combining Power Automate with Office Scripts is the ability to pass dynamic data between the two. Instead of writing scripts that are hardcoded for a single task or file, you can create reusable, flexible automations that respond to input—making your solutions more intelligent, adaptable, and scalable. Parameters turn a basic script into a powerful component in a larger, data-driven workflow.

Office Scripts support parameters in their main function, meaning you can send values from Power Automate directly into your script. For example, you might pass in a worksheet name, a specific cell address, or even a list of items gathered from a Microsoft Form, SharePoint list, or Teams message. This allows a single script to serve multiple purposes depending on the context.

Let's say you're building a flow that processes files as they arrive in a folder. Each file may contain a different report type, and you want the script to know which worksheet to update. In Power Automate, you can include a "Run script" action and pass a parameter like "RegionSummary" into the script. Then, in your script, your function would look like this:

```
function main(workbook: ExcelScript.Workbook,
sheetName: string) {
    let sheet = workbook.getWorksheet(sheetName);
    // process data as needed...
}
```

This flexibility is incredibly useful for workflows that need to scale. Instead of writing five different scripts to process five different report types, you write one well-structured script that takes a parameter and adapts its behaviour accordingly. You can also pass numeric values, Booleans, or arrays, depending on the complexity of your process.

Data can flow the other way as well. If your script performs a calculation, pulls a result from a cell, or generates a summary, you can return that value from the script to Power

Automate. This return data can then be used to populate an email, update a database, or trigger a conditional action elsewhere in the flow.

For instance, your script might calculate the total revenue from a dataset and return that figure. Power Automate could then use that number in a Teams notification: "This week's total sales exceeded $500,000." With a few lines of code and some simple flow design, your Excel automation becomes a fully integrated, real-time communication tool.

As you can see, passing parameters and data back and forth opens up endless possibilities for building smart, context-aware processes that go far beyond what VBA macros could ever do.

Passing Parameters and Data between Power Automate and Office Scripts

When you start passing parameters between Power Automate and Office Scripts, your automation moves from static to dynamic. Instead of creating multiple scripts for different files, reports, or workflows, you can build a single script that responds to data from the outside world. This not only simplifies your codebase but also allows you to integrate Excel automation into more sophisticated, real-time business processes.

Take a scenario where you collect regional sales reports from different offices. Each report includes the name of the region in its filename. Using Power Automate, you can extract that region name and pass it as a parameter to your Office Script. Inside the script, that region name can be used to filter data, label a worksheet, or determine where to insert the results. Here's how your main function might look:

Modern Excel Automation:

Migrating VBA Macros to Office Scripts and Power Automate

```
function main(workbook: ExcelScript.Workbook,
region: string) {
  const sheet =
workbook.getWorksheet("SalesData");
  const cell = sheet.getRange("A1");
  cell.setValue(`Processed Region: ${region}`);
}
```

In Power Automate, you'd set up a flow that captures the region from the file name (using a "Get file metadata" action or string manipulation), and then pass that region as a string to the script when calling the "Run script" action.

Likewise, Office Scripts can return values back to Power Automate. Suppose your script calculates the sum of all sales for that region. Instead of writing that total into the workbook, you might want to return it to Power Automate so it can be emailed, logged in a SharePoint list, or used to determine the next step in the flow. That return value can be referenced in later actions, like this:

```
function main(workbook: ExcelScript.Workbook):
number {
  const sheet =
workbook.getWorksheet("SalesData");
  const total = sheet.getRange("B2").getValue()
as number;
  return total;
}
```

This kind of two-way communication opens up endless possibilities. Your scripts become modular services that receive context, perform a task, and respond with useful results. And best of all, everything is handled in the background—automatically, accurately, and without needing someone to babysit Excel.

Once you're comfortable passing parameters and retrieving data, the next logical step is designing full-scale, automated flows. In the following section, we'll explore **scheduling scripts and building end-to-end workflows**, showing you how to run your Office Scripts on a schedule or tie them into complete business processes that run seamlessly across your Microsoft 365 environment.

Scheduling Scripts and Building End-to-End Workflows

One of the most transformative aspects of integrating Office Scripts with Power Automate is the ability to schedule scripts and connect them into complete, end-to-end workflows. With just a few clicks, you can automate tasks that used to take hours or rely on manual reminders—like updating reports, cleaning data, or distributing summaries—so they run automatically at specific times or in response to key business events.

Imagine a finance team that updates a revenue report every Monday morning. Traditionally, someone would open a file, run a macro, format the results, and email the output to stakeholders. Now, using Power Automate and Office Scripts, this process can be entirely hands-off. A scheduled flow runs every Monday at 6:00 a.m., launches an Office Script that pulls fresh data from linked sheets, recalculates summaries, formats the report, and even sends an Outlook email with the finished file attached—all without any user interaction.

These scheduled flows can be as simple or sophisticated as needed. You can chain multiple steps together: first refresh the data source, then run your Office Script, followed by conditional logic—such as sending an alert if sales fall below a certain threshold or uploading the output to a SharePoint document library for version tracking.

You can also design workflows that combine inputs from multiple systems. For instance, a manager submits a Microsoft Form with a custom request. That input feeds into Power Automate, which stores the request in a SharePoint list, passes parameters to an Office Script to update a workbook accordingly, and then confirms completion via Teams or email. It's not just automation—it's orchestration, with Excel acting as one part of a larger, intelligent flow.

Once your scripts are embedded in scheduled and responsive flows, your automations gain independence. They're no longer tied to a specific person running them, or to a desktop machine that must remain on. Everything runs in the background, in the cloud, across devices and teams.

To fully replace legacy automation models, the next step is understanding how to transition VBA-based scheduled tasks into this new system. In the following section, we'll look at how to **replace VBA scheduled tasks with automated flows**, making your Excel solutions more robust, scalable, and future-proof.

Replacing VBA Scheduled Tasks with Automated Flows

For years, many Excel power users have relied on scheduled VBA tasks to automate reporting, data cleanup, and file management. These automations often run through Windows Task Scheduler or custom add-ins, and while they've served their purpose well, they come with limitations. They're tied to a specific device, require Excel to be open at the right time, and can break if the user is logged out, if the network drive changes, or if a workbook isn't in the expected state. As organizations shift toward cloud-first infrastructure, these fragile, device-dependent tasks are becoming harder to maintain.

Power Automate offers a clean and modern alternative. By replacing VBA-based scheduled tasks with cloud flows, you eliminate reliance on physical machines and manual upkeep. For example, a VBA macro set to run every Friday morning at 7:00 a.m. to refresh a sales report can now be replaced with a scheduled flow in Power Automate that runs the Office Script at the exact same time—only now it's triggered from the cloud, doesn't require Excel to be open, and executes even if no user is online.

Imagine a legacy task where a macro opened a workbook, applied formatting, updated a chart, and emailed the file to department heads. That entire process can now be replicated in Power Automate. The flow can launch an Office Script to clean and format the workbook, save it in a SharePoint folder, and then use Outlook to send a customized email with a direct link to the updated file. What once required a dedicated machine and careful scheduling now becomes part of a seamless, reliable system.

Even better, these flows are easier to monitor and maintain. You can view their execution history, check logs for errors, and make changes without having to rewrite or debug lengthy VBA code. They're also more secure, since they follow Microsoft 365's identity and access management protocols, ensuring that only authorized users can trigger or modify them.

The transition from VBA to Power Automate isn't just a technical upgrade—it's a cultural one. It allows your automation to scale beyond the limits of individual users or departments and become part of a centralized, cloud-native ecosystem that supports collaboration and accountability.

Modern Excel Automation:

Migrating VBA Macros to Office Scripts and Power Automate

Now that we've replaced the old with the new, it's time to take automation even further. In the next chapter, we'll explore **advanced automation scenarios**, where Excel Online scripts interact with other services like SharePoint, Outlook, and Teams, and where your workflows can handle more complex, multi-user operations and external data sources.

10. Advanced Automation Scenarios

Once you've mastered the fundamentals of Office Scripts and Power Automate, a new world of possibilities opens up—where Excel is no longer just a spreadsheet tool, but a central part of an interconnected, intelligent automation system. These advanced scenarios allow you to build cross-platform solutions that connect Excel Online with external data, services, and users across your organization.

For example, consider a workflow that starts with a Microsoft Form submission. As soon as the form is filled out, Power Automate triggers a script that updates an Excel report with the new entry, recalculates KPIs, and posts a summary in a Teams channel. From there, an Outlook notification goes out to stakeholders with a chart attached, all completed automatically within seconds. No one opens Excel manually, no one runs macros, and yet the business stays informed and aligned.

You might also use Office Scripts to respond to structured data from external sources. Let's say your company receives CSV reports from vendors every week via OneDrive. A Power Automate flow can detect the new file, launch an Office Script to clean and transform the data, and insert it into a master Excel workbook. Instead of assigning someone to parse through spreadsheets manually, your automation does the work consistently, accurately, and on schedule.

As workflows become more sophisticated, they often need to serve multiple users. Advanced solutions might involve routing data to specific people based on their roles, sharing files through controlled SharePoint libraries, or capturing approvals through adaptive cards in Teams. All of this is possible by designing your scripts and flows with flexibility, security, and collaboration in mind.

The more you automate, the more you'll encounter edge cases, variations in file structures, and exceptions to handle. That's where conditional logic, error handling, and fallback strategies come in—making your workflows robust and resilient. And with logging tools and cloud monitoring, you can track execution history, debug issues, and optimize performance with ease.

Now that we're thinking beyond Excel and into integrated automation systems, the next step is to dive into **Combining Excel Online with Other Services** like SharePoint, Outlook, and Teams—unlocking full coordination between people, platforms, and data.

Combining Excel Online with Other Services (SharePoint, Outlook, Teams)

Modern business workflows rarely live in one application. Excel may be the hub for data, but it's the seamless interaction between Excel Online and other Microsoft 365 services—like SharePoint, Outlook, and Teams—that transforms automation from helpful to truly powerful. When these tools work together, you can create processes that are not only automatic but also collaborative, responsive, and deeply integrated into the way teams actually work.

Consider a monthly reporting process where department leads submit updates into Excel. Once the numbers are entered and validated through an Office Script, Power Automate takes over—saving the file to a SharePoint library, notifying the team via a customized Outlook email, and posting a summary message with highlights directly in a Teams channel. With one flow, your Excel script becomes part of a living, breathing communication and reporting system that touches everyone who needs to stay informed.

SharePoint integration is especially valuable for storing and versioning output files. Your Office Script can update a workbook in a document library, while Power Automate handles permissions, archives previous versions, and even initiates approval workflows if needed. Teams integration adds another layer—letting you notify the right group with links to updated reports, status alerts, or visual summaries pulled from your Excel data.

Outlook plays a key role in notifying stakeholders or confirming actions. After a script finishes formatting and analyzing a file, the flow can generate a dynamic email— automatically attaching the file, embedding a chart, or adding a personalized message based on the script's results. These messages aren't just notifications—they're extensions of your workflow that deliver the right data to the right people at the right time.

The result is an environment where data doesn't sit in a file— it moves, flows, and triggers collaboration. Excel becomes the engine, while SharePoint, Outlook, and Teams form the communication and control systems around it.

As your automations become more data-driven, you'll often need to pull in information from sources outside of Excel. In the next section, we'll explore **using Office Scripts to interact with external data**, including how to work with CSV and JSON files stored in OneDrive—so your workflows can process, transform, and integrate data from virtually anywhere.

Using Office Scripts to interact with external data (CSV/JSON via OneDrive)

One of the most valuable capabilities in advanced automation is the ability to bring external data into Excel without manual copying, pasting, or importing. With Office Scripts and OneDrive, you can streamline this process by automatically fetching and processing data stored in formats like CSV or JSON. These files might come from third-party services, internal applications, or other departments—and integrating them seamlessly into your Excel workflows turns static reports into dynamic, up-to-date dashboards.

Imagine your organization receives weekly product inventory data from a supplier in the form of a CSV file, which is automatically uploaded to a OneDrive folder. Instead of assigning someone to open the file and copy its contents into a master workbook, you can build a flow with Power Automate that triggers when a new file is added. That flow can launch an Office Script that opens your Excel workbook and pastes the cleaned data directly into a target worksheet.

Inside the script, you can structure the logic to remove unnecessary rows, validate column formats, or even merge the incoming data with existing tables. For example, the script might look for duplicates, append only new entries, or convert date strings into proper Excel date values. The flexibility here means you can shape the data exactly as you need it, without ever opening a file manually.

JSON files work similarly—especially useful when integrating with APIs or custom business systems. A Power Automate flow can retrieve JSON content, parse it, and pass specific elements as parameters to an Office Script. That script can then populate a worksheet with the extracted values, automatically build tables, or refresh charts. This is particularly effective for creating live reports that reflect data pulled from systems like CRMs, helpdesk platforms, or e-commerce dashboards.

By automating this process, you not only save time—you ensure accuracy and consistency. You also free your team from repetitive, low-value tasks so they can focus on analyzing data, not wrangling it.

As more people begin using these kinds of solutions, the next challenge is often coordination. In the following section, we'll look at how to build **multi-user and collaborative automation solutions**, where Office Scripts serve shared goals across teams, roles, and departments.

Multi-User and Collaborative Automation Solutions

As businesses grow more connected and teams become increasingly distributed, automation must do more than just complete tasks—it must support collaboration. With Office Scripts and Power Automate, it's now possible to build automation solutions that span departments, roles, and even time zones, all while remaining secure, scalable, and easy to maintain. These multi-user solutions enable teams to work together through shared workbooks, cloud flows, and centralized data sources—without ever getting in each other's way.

Consider a shared Excel workbook used by a project management team, where different users enter updates in designated sheets. An Office Script can be designed to run daily and consolidate all updates into a master dashboard. The script works behind the scenes, pulling each team's data into a central summary, color-coding based on progress, and refreshing key charts. Power Automate can then notify team leads in Teams or Outlook with a snapshot of current statuses. No one has to manually combine information, and everyone stays on the same page.

In another example, a finance department can collaborate with regional offices by maintaining a master budget workbook stored in SharePoint. Each region has its own worksheet or input form, and when updates are made, a script verifies the data and rolls it into a consolidated summary. If there's a discrepancy—like a missing approval or a formula error—the script flags the issue, and Power Automate can alert the correct user through Teams. This not only promotes accountability but also builds trust in the automation process itself.

These collaborative workflows are especially valuable because they're cloud-based. Everyone works in the same live workbook, with changes captured and processed in real time. Scripts are no longer limited to one person's machine—they belong to the team. Permissions can be managed through Microsoft 365, ensuring that the right people can trigger flows or view reports, while sensitive tasks remain secure and auditable.

Of course, there are still some limitations to be aware of— especially when scripts grow in complexity or when user interactions and external app integration are required. In the next section, we'll discuss the **limitations of Office Scripts and workarounds**, and when it's better to leverage Power Automate or Power Apps to achieve the best results in complex business scenarios.

Limitations of Office Scripts and Workarounds (when to use Power Automate or Power Apps)

As powerful as Office Scripts are for automating Excel Online, they aren't a one-size-fits-all solution. Like any tool, they come with limitations that may become apparent as your workflows grow in complexity, involve user interaction, or require integration with data sources beyond Excel. Understanding where Office Scripts excel—and where they fall short—can help you design smarter, more scalable automation by incorporating complementary tools like Power Automate and Power Apps.

One common limitation is user input. Unlike VBA, which allows for interactive forms, input boxes, or dialog windows, Office Scripts are designed to run automatically in the background. That means they can't ask the user to select a range or enter values mid-execution. If your automation requires dynamic input, Power Apps is often the better choice. You can build a simple form in Power Apps that gathers input from the user, then passes that information into an Office Script via Power Automate—bridging the gap between front-end interactivity and backend processing.

Another limitation is file handling. Office Scripts can only work with the currently open Excel workbook in the context of Excel Online. They can't open and manipulate multiple external workbooks within a single script. If your automation needs to pull data from several files stored in OneDrive or SharePoint, Power Automate becomes essential. You can use a flow to iterate through those files, extract the required data, and pass it one file at a time to an Office Script. This turns a single-script limitation into a manageable, scalable solution using the right combination of tools.

There are also performance considerations. Office Scripts work well with moderate amounts of data, but they may not be the best tool for processing extremely large datasets or running intensive loops. For those tasks, Power Automate can help by pre-filtering or preprocessing the data before it reaches Excel, or by using services like Power BI or Azure Functions when needed.

Lastly, error handling and debugging are more limited in Office Scripts compared to traditional development environments. There's no built-in debugger, and logs are relatively simple. This is where you might implement structured logging within your scripts or use Power Automate to capture and report error messages as part of the flow—such as emailing an admin if something fails or logging issues in a SharePoint list.

These limitations don't mean Office Scripts should be avoided—on the contrary, they remain a fast, accessible tool for many Excel automation tasks. But knowing when to extend them with Power Automate or pair them with Power Apps will help you design workflows that are both robust and future-ready.

To manage growing automation at scale, especially when it involves many flows and scripts, you'll want visibility into what's running, when, and how it's performing. In the next section, we'll explore **monitoring and logging in a cloud environment**, helping you build workflows that are not only smart but also easy to support and maintain over time.

Monitoring and Logging in a Cloud Environment

As your automations become more central to business operations, being able to monitor and log what's happening

Modern Excel Automation:

Migrating VBA Macros to Office Scripts and Power Automate

behind the scenes becomes essential. In traditional desktop-based automation—like with VBA—monitoring often involved manually checking files or building error messages into Excel cells. But in the cloud, especially when using Office Scripts and Power Automate, you have access to more robust, scalable ways to track, troubleshoot, and optimize your automated workflows.

With Office Scripts running as part of a Power Automate flow, every execution is recorded. You can see exactly when a script ran, whether it succeeded or failed, and how long it took. If something breaks—perhaps due to a missing file, permission issue, or formatting inconsistency—you can drill down into the flow history to pinpoint the step that failed. This level of insight makes it much easier to resolve issues without digging through lines of code or chasing down users for details.

In more advanced scenarios, you can build custom logging right into your automation. For example, an Office Script might write a summary of its actions (such as "25 rows imported," "2 duplicates removed," or "missing values in column C") into a dedicated worksheet. Meanwhile, a connected flow in Power Automate could push those details into a SharePoint list or Microsoft List, creating a live audit trail of what your scripts are doing over time. These logs can even trigger alerts—like emailing a team member when an error occurs, or posting to a Teams channel if data falls outside expected thresholds.

This kind of visibility turns your automation from a "black box" into a fully transparent process. You know what happened, when it happened, and why—without relying on someone to manually report problems. It's particularly useful when managing solutions across departments or when automating tasks that impact critical business functions.

Monitoring also helps with scaling. As you build more scripts and flows, having structured logs ensures you can maintain and improve your solutions without guesswork. Over time, these records become valuable assets—helping you identify usage patterns, detect inefficiencies, and justify automation ROI to stakeholders.

Now that we've explored how to build smart, integrated, and maintainable solutions, it's time to see how all of this works in the real world. In the next chapter, we'll dive into **real-world success stories**, showcasing how teams have transformed everything from finance reporting to inventory management and workflow modernization using Office Scripts and the Microsoft 365 ecosystem.

11. Real-World Success Stories

After exploring the tools, strategies, and techniques behind modern Excel automation, nothing brings the ideas to life quite like real-world success stories. These examples show how individuals and teams have moved beyond traditional spreadsheet habits and embraced cloud-based automation to solve practical business challenges. Whether streamlining reporting cycles, consolidating operational data, or connecting Excel with broader systems like SharePoint or Power BI, these stories demonstrate the true impact of combining Office Scripts with the Microsoft 365 platform.

Each scenario began with a familiar pain point—time-consuming manual processes, brittle VBA macros, or inefficient collaboration across teams. But by rethinking the approach and leveraging Office Scripts and Power Automate, those challenges were not only solved—they became opportunities to improve productivity, increase accuracy, and create automation that worked for everyone, not just advanced Excel users.

The power of these success stories lies in their accessibility. These are not enterprise-scale engineering efforts requiring massive investments. They're everyday automations built by analysts, operations leads, and finance professionals who recognized the potential in tools they already had access to. Their results have had a ripple effect—freeing up hours each week, reducing error rates, and helping organizations become more agile and data-driven.

In the next few sections, you'll see how a manual monthly finance process was transformed into a dynamic cloud-based dashboard, how inventory tracking was reimagined through SharePoint and Office Scripts, and how broader workflow modernization was achieved by bridging Excel with Power BI and automation flows.

Let's begin with the first story: a finance department's journey from a fragile macro-enabled workbook to a reliable, automated reporting system. In the next section, we'll explore **Case Study 1: Monthly Finance Report – From Macro Workbook to Cloud-Based Dashboard**.

Case Study 1: **Monthly Finance Report** – From Macro Workbook to Cloud-Based Dashboard

For years, the finance team at a mid-sized company relied on a heavily customized macro-enabled Excel workbook to produce their monthly financial report. The file was large, slow to open, and fragile—filled with legacy VBA code that only one team member truly understood. Every month, the same stressful cycle would begin: download raw data from accounting software, paste it into a hidden sheet, run the macro, hope it didn't crash, and then manually email the resulting report to a dozen stakeholders. If something changed in the data structure or a formula broke, the team often spent hours troubleshooting under tight deadlines.

Eventually, the team decided to modernize the process. Using Office Scripts and Excel Online, they restructured the workflow into a clean, modular automation that didn't rely on a single person or desktop environment. Raw data exports were automatically saved into a OneDrive folder. A scheduled Power Automate flow would trigger at the beginning of each month, launching an Office Script that cleaned and validated the data, applied consistent formatting, and inserted totals and KPIs into predefined sections of the workbook.

The updated workbook lived in SharePoint, so everyone accessed the same version. Once the report was complete, the flow posted a summary in a Teams channel and sent a personalized email via Outlook to each department head with a link to the final report and a visual chart embedded in the message. Everything happened in the cloud—fast, reliable, and version-controlled. And most importantly, it no longer depended on one person staying late at the end of each month to "fix the file again."

This transformation didn't just save time. It gave the finance team confidence in the accuracy of their numbers and allowed them to focus on analysis rather than cleanup. By moving away from a brittle macro and into a structured, automated, cloud-first process, they delivered faster insights with less effort and fewer errors.

Next, we'll shift from finance to operations and explore how another company streamlined their **inventory management process using Office Scripts and SharePoint**, reducing delays and gaining real-time visibility across locations.

Case Study 2: **Inventory Management –** Streamlining with Office Scripts and SharePoint

In a regional distribution company, inventory tracking was becoming increasingly difficult to manage as more warehouses came online. Each site maintained its own Excel file and updated stock levels manually. These files were emailed weekly to a central logistics coordinator, who would then copy-paste the data into a consolidated

Modern Excel Automation:

Migrating VBA Macros to Office Scripts and Power Automate

workbook. The process was tedious, prone to human error, and always a few days behind. It wasn't uncommon for discrepancies in quantities to go unnoticed until shipments were delayed or incorrect items were delivered.

To solve this, the company moved their inventory tracking system into a shared SharePoint environment. Each warehouse received its own standardized Excel Online template stored in a shared document library. The templates had protected sections and dropdowns for easy data entry, but the real magic happened behind the scenes. A Power Automate flow was created to run on a schedule, triggering an Office Script that extracted the latest data from each file and merged it into a central dashboard workbook—also stored in SharePoint.

The Office Script ensured that formatting was consistent, item codes were validated, and empty rows were ignored. The dashboard updated automatically every two hours, giving the logistics coordinator and management team near real-time visibility into stock levels across all locations. They no longer had to ask for weekly updates or deal with broken spreadsheets emailed in different formats. Everything was now centralized, accurate, and available on demand.

This change also empowered the warehouse teams. They no longer needed to worry about formatting or email chains. Their only responsibility was to enter data into their local file, knowing it would be picked up and processed automatically. Any issues—like missing entries or out-of-stock items—were flagged by the script and sent back to the respective team via a Teams message for review.

What started as a patchwork of spreadsheets evolved into a reliable system that scaled with the business and reduced both confusion and delays.

Next, we'll explore how a broader digital transformation was achieved by connecting Excel to even more powerful tools. In the following section, we'll look at **Case Study 3: Workflow Modernization – Integrating Excel with Power BI and Power Automate**, where Excel automation became part of a full analytics and reporting ecosystem.

Case Study 3: **Workflow Modernization – Integrating Excel with Power BI and Power Automate**

At a fast-growing services firm, project managers were spending hours every week preparing performance reports. Their process involved downloading data from a client portal, cleaning it in Excel, updating charts, and pasting key figures into PowerPoint slides for executive meetings. The task was repetitive, error-prone, and frustratingly disconnected from the firm's growing demand for real-time insights. Leaders wanted fresher data and fewer delays, but the existing workflow wasn't built to scale.

The turning point came when the team decided to rethink the entire process using Office Scripts, Power Automate, and Power BI. They started by redesigning the Excel file structure—simplifying data inputs, removing manual steps, and enabling automated updates through Office Scripts. Each project manager saved a copy of the standardized template to SharePoint, where the latest project data was stored and regularly refreshed.

Power Automate stepped in to handle orchestration. A flow was created to monitor for file updates, automatically run the Office Script to clean and validate data, and then export the cleaned results to a dataset in Power BI. Within minutes, the data appeared in visual dashboards that were accessible to executives through a browser or mobile device—no more chasing people down for status reports or waiting for the next PowerPoint.

The team also added logic to send automated alerts via Teams if certain thresholds were met—for example, if a project went over budget or a milestone was delayed. These notifications were based on calculations performed in Excel and pushed into Power BI and Teams via the same automated pipeline.

The impact was immediate. Project managers saved time every week, executives had access to live data without requesting updates, and the team could finally focus on strategy instead of formatting. The integration of Excel, Power BI, and Power Automate turned a scattered reporting task into a living, responsive system that evolved with the business.

But no transformation comes without a few bumps along the way. In the next section, we'll take a candid look at **Lessons Learned: Common Pitfalls and How to Avoid Them**, so you can build your automation projects with clarity, confidence, and fewer surprises.

Lessons Learned: Common Pitfalls and How to Avoid Them

Every automation journey comes with its fair share of lessons—and the path from traditional VBA macros to modern, cloud-first Office Scripts is no different. While the shift opens doors to speed, scalability, and collaboration, it also introduces new ways of thinking that can trip up even experienced Excel users. Fortunately, many of the common challenges can be avoided with a bit of foresight and some thoughtful planning.

Modern Excel Automation:

Migrating VBA Macros to Office Scripts and Power Automate

One of the most frequent pitfalls is treating Office Scripts like a direct VBA replacement. While they share some functional overlap, the environment, structure, and purpose of Office Scripts are fundamentally different. A script that relies heavily on selecting ranges, activating sheets, or interacting with users mid-execution may work in VBA but fail in Excel Online. The most successful migrations come from reimagining—not replicating—workflows, keeping in mind the strengths of the cloud environment.

Another challenge appears when scripts are built quickly without attention to maintainability. In the excitement of getting a working result, it's easy to hardcode values, skip commenting, or overlook structure. But over time, these shortcuts add up. When something breaks or needs to scale, you'll wish for cleaner logic and better documentation. Teams that invested early in naming conventions, clear functions, and modular code found it far easier to maintain and evolve their scripts across projects.

Performance is another area that catches people off guard. Unlike local Excel, where instant feedback is the norm, scripts running in Excel Online—especially through Power Automate—can have delays or timeouts if they process too much data inefficiently. Early adopters often learn to optimize their code by minimizing unnecessary calls to the workbook and processing data in memory whenever possible.

Finally, communication between team members can be a weak link. When automations are shared but not documented—or when only one person understands how a flow works—it creates risk. Successful teams made it a habit to use shared workspaces, version-controlled scripts, and centralized dashboards so everyone could understand what was running, when, and why.

Modern Excel Automation:

Migrating VBA Macros to Office Scripts and Power Automate

These lessons don't just come from technical issues—they're reminders that automation is about people as much as code. The smoother the collaboration, the more sustainable the solution becomes.

As you look ahead and build automations meant to last, it's helpful to follow proven practices that will keep your solutions secure, maintainable, and scalable. In the next chapter, we'll explore **Best Practices for Future-Proof Excel Solutions**, including security, performance optimization, version control, and collaboration tips to help your Excel workflows stand the test of time.

12. Best Practices for Future-Proof Excel Solutions

Building automation in Excel isn't just about solving today's problems—it's about creating workflows that will continue to serve your team as business needs evolve. Future-proofing your Excel solutions means designing with sustainability, scalability, and collaboration in mind. Whether you're writing Office Scripts, designing flows in Power Automate, or managing shared workbooks in the cloud, the decisions you make today will determine how easy—or difficult—it will be to maintain your solutions tomorrow.

One of the key habits shared by teams who succeed long term is thinking modularly. They don't just write scripts that solve one specific use case—they build flexible logic that can be reused or expanded when new data types or departments come into the picture. For example, a script that summarizes data from a worksheet might accept dynamic parameters for sheet names or cell ranges. This small adjustment can save hours of rework down the road when a new region or report format is added to the workflow.

Documentation and code clarity also play a critical role. It's easy to assume that you'll remember what each part of your script does—but future you, or the teammate who inherits the solution, may not be so lucky. Adding clear comments, separating logic into functions, and maintaining a changelog help create automation that feels like a shared asset rather than a personal tool. Teams that include these practices from the start are far better equipped to grow and support their automations over time.

Equally important is cross-functional collaboration. Future-proof solutions are rarely built in isolation. They involve IT, operations, analysts, and sometimes even HR or legal—especially when automation touches sensitive or regulated data. A well-designed Excel solution is one that lives in the cloud, is easily accessible to stakeholders, and follows governance rules that ensure both flexibility and security.

And of course, nothing stays static in tech. Microsoft 365 evolves rapidly, with new features in Excel Online, Power Automate, and the Office Scripts API rolling out all the time. Staying current means tapping into the community, exploring learning hubs, and attending the occasional webinar or user group. The tools will keep changing—but your ability to adapt will keep your solutions relevant and impactful.

With this mindset in place, it's time to dive into one of the most foundational aspects of future-proofing: **Security and Governance for Office Scripts**. In the next section, we'll explore how to manage admin controls, permissions, and policies to ensure your automation remains safe, compliant, and aligned with your organization's broader IT strategy.

Security and Governance for Office Scripts (Admin Controls, Permissions)

As Office Scripts become more widely adopted across organizations, it's essential to ensure that automation is not only efficient but also secure and compliant. Unlike traditional VBA macros, which typically run locally and have limited oversight, Office Scripts operate in a cloud environment—integrated with OneDrive, SharePoint, and Power Automate. This opens up powerful new capabilities, but it also introduces important questions about control, access, and accountability.

A good governance strategy begins with understanding who has the ability to create and run scripts. Microsoft 365 provides admin settings that allow IT teams to enable or disable Office Scripts at the tenant level. For organizations that want to roll out automation gradually, this level of control helps limit access to power users or specific departments while still allowing experimentation in sandbox environments. For example, a company might allow the finance and analytics teams to use Office Scripts while restricting access for departments handling sensitive HR data.

Permissions also play a major role in how scripts are used. Since scripts can modify workbooks, it's important that users only run automations on documents they're authorized to access. SharePoint and OneDrive provide document-level access controls, ensuring that data isn't exposed or altered by mistake. Combined with version history, these safeguards allow teams to collaborate safely—even when automating tasks across files owned by multiple users.

For workflows that involve multiple people or departments, clear script ownership is key. Establishing shared folders for scripts, naming conventions that include author initials or creation dates, and storing documentation alongside the scripts all contribute to responsible automation. If a script triggers a data change or fails unexpectedly, having clear visibility into who built it, where it's stored, and how it works can prevent confusion and downtime.

In highly regulated industries, auditability is crucial. Power Automate complements Office Scripts by maintaining detailed logs of when flows run, who triggered them, and whether any errors occurred. This kind of traceability not only helps with troubleshooting—it can also satisfy compliance requirements for industries like finance, healthcare, or government.

By combining Office Scripts with strong governance
practices, teams can embrace automation confidently,
knowing their tools are aligned with company policies and
security standards.

With your scripts secure and well-managed, the next step is
making sure they run as efficiently as possible. In the
following section, we'll explore **Optimizing Performance in
Office Scripts vs. VBA**, helping you get the most out of
every line of code—whether you're cleaning data, building
reports, or scaling automation across your team.

Optimizing Performance in Office Scripts vs. VBA

When comparing Office Scripts with traditional VBA,
performance isn't just about speed—it's about reliability,
scalability, and how efficiently your code interacts with data.
While VBA runs directly within the Excel desktop
environment and can feel faster for small, localized tasks,
Office Scripts—executed in the cloud—offer powerful
advantages when optimized properly. That said, the shift
from desktop to online scripting comes with a few key
differences that every developer should understand to get
the best performance out of their solutions.

One of the most important concepts in Office Scripts is
minimizing workbook interaction. Unlike VBA, which can
update a cell and instantly reflect the change, Office Scripts
run in a more structured, batch-oriented manner. Each call
to get or set a range value involves communication between
the script and the workbook object model. That means
frequent back-and-forth operations—like looping through
each row to update one cell at a time—can slow down your
script significantly.

Modern Excel Automation:

Migrating VBA Macros to Office Scripts and Power Automate

The smarter approach is to work with arrays whenever possible. For example, instead of writing a value to 100 rows one at a time, you can load the entire range into memory, process your data in JavaScript-style arrays, and write it back in a single action. This reduces communication overhead and speeds up execution dramatically. It's a small shift in mindset for someone used to VBA's procedural flow but makes a huge difference in large datasets.

Another advantage of Office Scripts is their ability to scale in shared environments. Since scripts can be triggered through Power Automate and run on cloud infrastructure, they don't rely on a user's machine or Excel instance being open. However, this also means you need to plan for execution limits and occasional throttling, especially in high-traffic scenarios. Keeping scripts clean, focused, and modular improves performance and reduces the chance of unexpected slowdowns.

VBA still holds advantages for certain local, UI-driven tasks—such as creating interactive forms or responding to real-time events like a user clicking a button. But when it comes to automating scheduled tasks, handling structured data transformations, and running in a secure, multi-user environment, Office Scripts shine—especially when the code is well-optimized for the online model.

Now that your scripts are running efficiently, it's time to think about how to manage them over time. In the next section, we'll dive into **Maintaining and Versioning Office Script Code**, so you can keep your automation clean, consistent, and easy to update as your needs evolve.

Maintaining and Versioning Office Script Code

Writing a script that works is only the beginning. As business processes evolve and teams grow, maintaining and versioning your Office Script code becomes just as important as writing it in the first place. What starts as a simple one-person automation can quickly turn into a critical tool used across departments—so having a plan for keeping your code clean, up to date, and traceable is essential for long-term success.

One of the best ways to maintain scripts is to treat them like living documentation. That means writing meaningful comments inside the script—not just what the code is doing, but why it's doing it that way. For instance, if you're skipping over blank rows or using a fallback worksheet name, explain the reasoning. This becomes especially helpful when you or a teammate returns to the script months later and needs to debug or expand it.

Consistent naming conventions are also key. Naming your scripts descriptively (like updateQuarterlySalesDashboard or mergeInventoryFromRegionSheets) makes them easier to locate and understand. When you're dealing with dozens of scripts across projects, meaningful names help you and your team avoid mistakes and navigate with confidence.

Versioning is another powerful habit. While Excel Online doesn't offer built-in version control for scripts yet, you can manage versions manually by saving dated or numbered copies with notes on what changed. Some teams use a SharePoint document library or OneNote page to keep a changelog with links to each version. Others export and save script code as .txt or .ts files in a Git repository or OneDrive folder. These small steps can prevent bigger problems later—like accidentally overwriting a working script or not being able to undo a faulty edit.

Also, when you're working on a major update or redesign, consider duplicating the script and working on a draft version until it's fully tested. This reduces risk, especially in production environments where the script might be tied to live workflows in Power Automate or shared Excel files.

By managing your scripts with care, you set yourself—and your collaborators—up for success. Well-maintained code builds trust, minimizes errors, and saves hours of rework down the line.

And speaking of collaboration, the next section focuses on just that. We'll explore **Tips for Team Collaboration on Excel Online Automation**, including how to build shared workflows, organize script libraries, and ensure smooth teamwork in the cloud.

Tips for Team Collaboration on Excel Online Automation

Automation works best when it's built as a shared resource, not a solo effort. Excel Online, combined with Office Scripts and Power Automate, opens the door for true collaboration—where teams can co-develop, test, and manage automations together without stepping on each other's toes. But as more people get involved, working smoothly as a team requires thoughtful habits and a bit of structure.

One of the most helpful practices is organizing your scripts in a shared environment. Instead of storing scripts in personal OneDrive accounts, use shared SharePoint folders or team-based workspaces where everyone can access, review, and contribute to the code. This setup not only makes your work more transparent but also reduces the risk of key scripts getting lost or locked away in someone's private storage. For example, a marketing team that runs weekly campaign summaries might keep all related scripts in a shared "Reports Automation" library alongside the source files and documentation.

Clarity is just as important as access. When multiple people are editing or reviewing scripts, descriptive naming conventions and comments become essential. Each script should have a clear purpose, and if it's tied to a Power Automate flow, note that in the script itself or in a team log. Something as simple as adding the line // Used in weekly reporting flow triggered by SharePoint upload can save teammates a lot of time when tracing errors or figuring out dependencies.

Communication plays a big role too. Collaborative automation thrives when teams share not just files, but ideas. Holding regular check-ins or "automation hours" where team members present their workflows, challenges, or new script ideas can spark inspiration and reduce duplication of effort. These moments also give newer users the chance to learn from others and become more confident contributing to the team's automation toolkit.

And when issues do arise—as they inevitably do—a shared troubleshooting log or internal help channel (like a Teams chat) can speed up resolution and prevent repeated mistakes. For instance, if a script failed because a data range shifted, noting that in a team log helps others avoid the same oversight.

Ultimately, successful collaboration in Excel Online automation comes down to making your scripts discoverable, understandable, and easy to build on. When teams work from a shared foundation, innovation tends to happen faster—and with fewer surprises.

In the final section of this chapter, we'll explore how to keep growing as Excel automation evolves. Let's look at **Keeping Skills Up-to-Date: Learning Resources and Community**, and where to find support, inspiration, and best practices in the ever-expanding Microsoft ecosystem.

Keeping Skills Up-to-Date: Learning Resources and Community

In the fast-moving world of Excel automation, staying current is one of the most valuable habits you can build. Office Scripts, Power Automate, and the broader Microsoft 365 ecosystem are evolving constantly—with new features, integrations, and best practices emerging all the time. Fortunately, the Excel automation community is active, generous, and filled with resources that make learning both accessible and enjoyable.

One of the most effective ways to keep your skills sharp is by following real-world examples. Microsoft's official documentation offers step-by-step guides and sample scripts, but some of the most creative solutions come from user blogs, GitHub repositories, and community forums. Whether you're trying to optimize script performance, troubleshoot a complex flow, or build a reusable framework, chances are someone else has asked a similar question— or shared a clever solution.

For many professionals, subscribing to newsletters, LinkedIn groups, or YouTube channels focused on Excel and automation becomes a weekly routine. These resources often spotlight updates before they roll out widely, helping you stay ahead of changes that could affect your scripts or flows. For example, knowing that Power Automate recently added new connectors or that Office Scripts now supports additional object types can spark ideas for how to improve or expand existing workflows.

Another valuable resource is the Microsoft Tech Community and the Office Scripts tag on the Power Automate forums. These platforms are more than just Q&A hubs—they're places where developers, analysts, and business users exchange insights, showcase solutions, and help troubleshoot one another's work. Participating in these communities not only accelerates your learning but connects you with like-minded professionals facing similar challenges.

And if you're part of a larger organization, internal learning groups or automation clubs can help create a culture of continuous growth. Teams that dedicate even a little time each month to share what they've learned, explore new features, or run mini-hackathons often find that their automation maturity advances much faster than expected.

Most importantly, learning in this space isn't about mastering it all—it's about staying curious. Whether you're deep into TypeScript, just starting with Power Automate, or somewhere in between, there's always something new to explore.

With that spirit of ongoing discovery, we now reach the final chapter. In **Conclusion and Next Steps**, we'll reflect on what the journey from VBA to Office Scripts means in practice, how it's transforming business workflows, and where the future of Excel automation is headed—including the exciting possibilities with AI and beyond.

13. Conclusion and Next Steps

Reaching the end of this journey doesn't mean the end of your learning—it marks the beginning of a new chapter in how you approach Excel, automation, and business efficiency. What started with macros and manual routines has now evolved into a cloud-first, collaborative environment where automations run reliably, scale effortlessly, and connect seamlessly with the broader Microsoft 365 ecosystem. The shift from VBA to Office Scripts isn't just about code—it's about mindset, adaptability, and preparing for a future where automation is no longer a technical luxury, but a professional necessity.

Throughout this transformation, what stands out most is the empowerment it brings. A finance analyst no longer needs to rely on IT to maintain complex macros. A project manager can set up reports that run like clockwork. A small business owner can scale operations using tools already available in Microsoft 365—all without needing to become a full-time developer. These are real changes that improve real workflows, and the ripple effect across teams, departments, and entire organizations is already being felt.

The most exciting part? This space is still growing. New features in Office Scripts and Power Automate are arriving frequently. Integration with AI services like Copilot is beginning to redefine how we build and use scripts. Even now, we're just scratching the surface of what's possible with data-driven decision-making, intelligent automation, and human-centric design working in harmony.

Wherever you are on this journey—whether you've just started migrating macros or you're designing enterprise-wide flows—the key is to keep moving forward. Keep experimenting. Keep sharing what you build. And most of all, keep looking for opportunities to replace repetitive work with smarter, faster, and more resilient solutions.

To help ground everything you've learned, let's begin this final chapter with a quick **Recap of Key Takeaways from VBA to Office Scripts Migration**, highlighting the major shifts, lessons, and benefits covered throughout this book.

Recap of Key Takeaways from VBA to Office Scripts Migration

Looking back on the migration from VBA to Office Scripts, it's clear that the change is more than just technical—it represents a shift in how we think about automation, access, and agility in the modern workplace. Where VBA once provided powerful desktop-level automation, Office Scripts extends that power to the cloud, making automation accessible, scalable, and collaborative in entirely new ways.

At its core, the transition brings a fundamental benefit: automation is no longer bound to a single user or device. A sales report that once depended on a macro stored on one person's laptop can now run automatically in the cloud, triggered by a file upload or a scheduled flow, and delivered in real time to a whole team. That alone can transform how people work—eliminating bottlenecks, reducing errors, and freeing time for more valuable tasks.

Throughout this migration, we've also seen that success comes from more than just translating code. It requires rethinking workflows to match the strengths of Excel Online, using Power Automate to build connections between systems, and applying good coding practices like modular design, meaningful naming, and clear version control.

Organizations that took time to rebuild with intention—not just replicate old macros—unlocked far greater value in the process.

And while Office Scripts may not yet match VBA in every technical feature, especially for UI-driven tasks, it excels in areas that matter most for modern operations: cloud accessibility, seamless integration, automation scheduling, and improved governance. Teams that previously struggled with conflicting versions, unreliable macros, or manual reporting now run clean, consistent processes without a single mouse click.

This evolution also opens the door for broader collaboration. Automation no longer lives in silos—it becomes something shared, scalable, and understandable by entire teams. That cultural shift, paired with the right tools, lays the foundation for long-term innovation.

Now that we've revisited the key lessons and milestones of this transformation, it's time to explore what all of this means for your organization as a whole. In the next section, we'll take a closer look at **The Business Impact of Cloud-Based Excel Automation**, and how it's driving measurable results across industries and teams.

The Business Impact of Cloud-Based Excel Automation

The move to cloud-based Excel automation is more than just a technical upgrade—it's a business decision with far-reaching consequences. When organizations adopt Office Scripts and Power Automate, they're not just replacing old macros; they're redefining how work gets done. And the impact is tangible. Teams become faster, data becomes

Modern Excel Automation:

Migrating VBA Macros to Office Scripts and Power Automate

cleaner, and insights flow more freely across the organization.

Consider the difference in a typical reporting cycle. A manual process that once required exporting CSV files, copying data into a spreadsheet, running a macro, and manually emailing results might have taken hours each week. Now, that entire workflow can be triggered automatically the moment a file lands in a SharePoint folder. The latest data is cleaned, visualized, and shared without a single manual touch. This kind of automation doesn't just save time—it builds consistency and trust in the process.

Cloud-based automation also improves transparency. With flows running in Power Automate and scripts executing on Excel Online, every action is tracked. Teams can view when a script ran, who triggered it, and whether it completed successfully. This visibility is especially important for compliance-driven industries like finance or healthcare, where audit trails and data governance matter just as much as the results themselves.

There's also the scalability factor. Traditional macros often lived on one user's device, and scaling them across departments could be risky or inconsistent. But cloud-based automation can be built once and reused across regions, projects, or teams, all while staying under IT control. For example, a standardized budgeting tool built with Office Scripts can be deployed to regional teams through SharePoint, with each team feeding data into a centralized dashboard—allowing executives to view global performance in real time.

Most importantly, cloud automation empowers users. When people across departments can build or adapt solutions without waiting for developers, innovation spreads. It frees up IT teams to focus on strategic projects while business users solve everyday challenges more efficiently. That's the kind of impact that improves not only workflows but workplace culture as a whole.

With all this value unlocked, it's important to stay forward-thinking. In the next section, we'll look at how to maintain that momentum through **Encouragement for Continuous Improvement and Innovation**—because the journey doesn't end when a process is automated. That's when the real transformation begins.

Encouragement for Continuous Improvement and Innovation

One of the greatest strengths of cloud-based Excel automation is that it's never truly finished—and that's a good thing. The ability to continuously improve, adapt, and innovate is what turns a simple script into a long-term strategic asset. The most successful teams treat automation not as a one-time fix but as an evolving part of their daily workflow, constantly asking: how can this be faster, clearer, or more useful?

Innovation often starts small. It might be the moment someone automates a weekly email summary instead of sending it manually. Or when a script that was built to clean one worksheet is rewritten to handle an entire folder of reports. These small wins not only boost productivity but also inspire confidence in the tools and in the people using them. One organization even went a step further by creating an internal "automation wall of fame" where team members could showcase their solutions, from error-checking forms to fully automated reporting flows. It sparked a culture of curiosity, where employees actively looked for ways to improve and share their ideas.

But continuous improvement isn't just about making existing automations better. It's also about keeping your eyes open to what's newly possible. As Microsoft continues to expand the Office Scripts API and enhance Power Automate's capabilities, opportunities emerge that didn't exist even six months ago. Staying engaged—whether through community events, webinars, or simply exploring new actions in Power Automate—keeps your automation mindset fresh and your solutions relevant.

Importantly, innovation doesn't have to come from technical experts alone. Often, the best ideas come from the people closest to the process—those who understand the pain points, the timing, and the data firsthand. By encouraging collaboration between business users and technical teams, companies can unlock creative solutions that are both practical and scalable.

In the next section, we'll take a look at what's ahead. From new features on the Office Scripts roadmap to AI-enhanced workflows in Excel, the tools are evolving rapidly—and so are the possibilities. Let's explore **Exploring Next Horizons: Office Scripts roadmap, AI and Excel automation**, and see where the future is headed.

Exploring Next Horizons: Office Scripts roadmap, AI and Excel automation

As we look to the future of Excel automation, it's clear that we're only beginning to tap into what's possible. Office Scripts has already reshaped how we automate workflows in Excel Online, but the next chapter promises to be even more transformative. With continued updates from Microsoft, deeper integration with the broader Microsoft 365 platform, and the rapid rise of AI, the future of Excel automation is not

Modern Excel Automation:

Migrating VBA Macros to Office Scripts and Power Automate

only more powerful—it's more intelligent, more collaborative, and more human-centric than ever before.

One area seeing exciting development is the Office Scripts API itself. With each release, new methods and objects are being added, allowing scripts to interact more deeply with tables, charts, PivotTables, and even more workbook events. For instance, scenarios that once required complicated workarounds—like dynamically formatting data or generating multiple sheets based on categories—are becoming easier to implement with native script capabilities. As the language grows, so does the range of problems it can solve.

Meanwhile, AI is rapidly becoming a co-pilot in automation. Tools like Microsoft 365 Copilot and Power Automate's AI builder are enabling users to describe what they want in natural language, then generate script scaffolding or flow suggestions automatically. This lowers the barrier to entry for new users and accelerates development for experienced ones. A data analyst who once spent hours writing a script to parse survey responses can now describe the desired outcome, let AI generate the base, and fine-tune it manually—a workflow that's not just efficient but empowering.

The convergence of Excel with other platforms like Power BI, Power Apps, and Teams also means that automation is no longer confined to spreadsheets. It's now about creating connected experiences—where Excel is the engine, but the impact is felt across dashboards, chatbots, forms, and mobile apps. A script that updates a financial summary might also refresh a Power BI tile and post a summary in a Teams channel, all within the same automated pipeline. This holistic approach turns Excel into a living part of the business infrastructure.

The best part? You don't need to be a developer to start taking advantage of these tools. The future belongs to curious problem-solvers—those willing to explore, test, and build. Whether you're automating your first spreadsheet or managing an enterprise-wide rollout, staying engaged with what's next will keep your skills sharp and your solutions relevant.

To help you continue that journey, the final section of this book includes **Additional Resources and Further Reading**, offering trusted sources, learning paths, and communities to keep your momentum going long after the last page.

Additional Resources and Further Reading

Even though this book is coming to a close, your journey with Office Scripts, Power Automate, and modern Excel automation is just beginning. The tools you've explored here are part of a dynamic and rapidly evolving ecosystem—one that rewards curiosity, community, and continual learning. Fortunately, there's no shortage of high-quality resources to support you as you deepen your skills and tackle new challenges.

For hands-on learners, Microsoft's official documentation offers a solid foundation. The Office Scripts documentation includes beginner tutorials and advanced use cases, while the Power Automate learning paths guide you through building flows step by step. If you're the kind of person who likes to tinker with real-world examples, GitHub repositories and Microsoft's Tech Community are filled with shared scripts, templates, and use cases from professionals around the world.

Modern Excel Automation:

Migrating VBA Macros to Office Scripts and Power Automate

Another excellent way to stay current is to follow experts in the Excel and Power Platform communities on LinkedIn, YouTube, or blogs. Many of them break down complex concepts into practical videos, walkthroughs, and articles that are easier to digest than formal documentation. For instance, watching someone build and debug a live Office Script is often more insightful than reading about it—and it helps bridge the gap between theory and practice.

Live events, webinars, and user groups (both virtual and in-person) are also great spaces for inspiration. Participating in monthly Power Platform community calls or Excel training events can give you early access to new features, help you ask questions in real time, and connect with like-minded professionals who are solving similar problems.

If your organization is embracing automation across teams, consider setting up an internal knowledge hub or automation channel where colleagues can share what they've learned, post code snippets, or ask for feedback. These shared learning environments not only accelerate adoption—they create a culture of experimentation and shared ownership of automation success.

To help you continue exploring on your own terms, the final part of this book includes several appendices filled with handy references, side-by-side object comparisons, syntax shortcuts, and ready-to-use tools. In **Appendices**, you'll find everything from VBA-to-Office Scripts mappings, cheat sheets, templates, and even a glossary to keep new terms and concepts at your fingertips whenever you need them.

Appendices

Appendix A: Quick Reference – VBA Objects vs. Office Scripts Objects

One of the most common questions from Excel users transitioning from VBA to Office Scripts is, "Where did all my objects go?" While Office Scripts and VBA are built around similar concepts—like workbooks, worksheets, ranges, and tables—the way they express and interact with these elements is quite different. This appendix offers a quick-reference bridge between the two, helping you recognize familiar structures in a new language and avoid getting lost in translation.

In VBA, much of the syntax is intuitive once you're used to it. You might write Worksheets("Sheet1").Range("A1").Value = "Hello" and understand exactly what's happening. In Office Scripts, the same idea uses a more object-oriented and asynchronous approach, such as:

```
workbook.getWorksheet("Sheet1").getRange("A1").
setValue("Hello");
```
The functionality is identical—but the flow is different. You're explicitly getting a worksheet, accessing a range from that worksheet, and then setting a value using a method call. It's more structured, and that structure becomes even more helpful as your automations grow in complexity.

Another shift is how collections are handled. In VBA, a loop through all worksheets might look like For Each ws In Worksheets. In Office Scripts, it becomes workbook.getWorksheets().forEach(...). Again, same intent—new rhythm. The methods in Office Scripts give you predictable, chainable behavior that makes code more readable and maintainable, especially when working with cloud data sources or integrating with Power Automate.

And while the object names often differ slightly (e.g., Range vs. RangeArea, Cells vs. getCell(row, column)), the logic behind them remains familiar. You'll still define variables, loop through rows, write formulas, and sort tables—but you'll be doing it in a way that aligns with modern scripting standards and best practices.

Think of this reference not as a dictionary, but as a translator between two generations of automation. Once you're comfortable with the Office Scripts equivalents, you'll find that many of your VBA patterns carry over surprisingly well— just with a cleaner, more modular twist.

In the next section—**Appendix B: Office Scripts Syntax Cheat Sheet for VBA Developers**—you'll find a compact, ready-to-use guide that pairs common VBA commands with their Office Scripts counterparts, so you can look up exactly what you need when writing or converting code.

Appendix B: Office Scripts Syntax Cheat Sheet for VBA Developers

For anyone who has spent years writing VBA macros, diving into Office Scripts can feel a bit like switching dialects—you recognize the words, but the sentence structure is different. This cheat sheet is designed to make that transition smoother by mapping familiar VBA commands to their modern Office Scripts equivalents.

Let's start with something basic. A classic VBA line that writes a value into a cell looks like this:

```
Range("B2").Value = "Report Complete"
```
In Office Scripts, the same action becomes:

```
worksheet.getRange("B2").setValue("Report
Complete");
```
The logic is nearly identical—you're still targeting cell B2 and inserting a string. But in Office Scripts, every action is done through explicit method calls, which makes the structure more consistent and predictable across different objects.

Working with loops is another area where Office Scripts shines once you get the hang of it. In VBA, looping through rows might look like:

```
For i = 1 To 10
    Cells(i, 1).Value = i
Next i
```
The Office Scripts equivalent uses JavaScript-style loops and methods:

```
for (let i = 0; i < 10; i++) {
    worksheet.getCell(i, 0).setValue(i + 1);
}
```
You'll notice that indexing starts at 0 instead of 1, which is a core part of JavaScript and TypeScript logic. Once this becomes second nature, your code becomes more adaptable to broader programming environments, and your logic gets easier to integrate into cloud-based workflows.

Another helpful translation is for handling tables. In VBA, you might write:

```
ListObjects("SalesData").Range.AutoFilter
```
In Office Scripts:

```
worksheet.getTable("SalesData").applyAutoFilter
();
```
It's straightforward, but the structure always begins with the workbook or worksheet, then drills into the object you're

targeting. Everything is method-based, which not only improves code readability but also ensures a more consistent experience when integrating with tools like Power Automate.

This cheat sheet is meant to be something you can return to again and again—whether you're rewriting old macros or building new scripts from scratch. Keep it handy when you're not quite sure how to translate your VBA knowledge into the Office Scripts world, and over time, the new syntax will start to feel just as natural as the old.

In the next section, we'll look at real-world tools to help accelerate your automation journey. **Appendix C: Useful Tools and Templates** includes time-saving code snippets, ready-made Power Automate templates, and reusable logic blocks to help you go from idea to solution even faster.

Appendix C: Useful Tools and Templates (Code snippets, Power Automate templates)

One of the best ways to accelerate your work with Office Scripts and Power Automate is by reusing what already works. Whether you're new to scripting or just want to save time, having a library of proven code snippets and ready-made templates can dramatically reduce the time it takes to build and deploy automations. This appendix gathers some of the most practical, real-world tools to help you move faster while staying consistent and organized.

Let's begin with a few versatile Office Scripts snippets. These are the kinds of building blocks that appear in countless automations. For instance, if you frequently work with data imports and need to clear a worksheet before loading new information, the following snippet does exactly that:

```
let sheet = workbook.getWorksheet("ImportData");
sheet.getUsedRange().clear();
```

It's clean, fast, and avoids the risk of leftover data contaminating your new results. Another popular snippet is used to loop through all rows of a table and apply formatting or calculations:

```
let table = workbook.getTable("Sales");
let dataRange = table.getDataBodyRange();
let rowCount = dataRange.getRowCount();

for (let i = 0; i < rowCount; i++) {
    let cell = dataRange.getCell(i, 3); // Assume column 4 has total values
    cell.setNumberFormat("$#,##0.00");
}
```

This type of code is common when you want to ensure all numeric data appears clean and professional before exporting or sharing reports.

On the Power Automate side, templates make it easy to create sophisticated workflows without starting from scratch. A favorite among users is a flow that triggers when a file is added to a SharePoint folder, runs an Office Script to process the data, then emails a summary to a team. By saving this flow as a template, you can duplicate and adapt it for different projects—such as importing survey results, refreshing dashboards, or generating invoices.

Another valuable template connects Excel Online with Teams and Outlook. For example, after a script updates a tracker with new KPIs, the flow can post the results directly into a Teams channel and send a formatted summary to leadership. This eliminates the need for manual follow-ups and ensures your team is always aligned with the latest data.

If you're building your own library of snippets and flows, consider storing them in a shared document library or GitHub repo with notes on when and how to use each one. This way, colleagues can quickly discover and contribute to a growing collection of solutions, turning automation into a shared asset instead of a personal project.

These templates and code samples are just a starting point—but they reflect the kind of practical automation that saves time, reduces error, and scales across your organization. And as you build your own solutions, don't hesitate to tweak, remix, or combine them into workflows uniquely suited to your team's needs.

To help you keep track of key concepts along the way, the final appendix provides clear, jargon-free definitions of the most important terms you've encountered in this book. In **Appendix D: Glossary of Terms**, you'll find concise explanations of everything from Excel Online and Office Scripts to Power Automate, connectors, triggers, actions, and more—so you can confidently navigate both technical conversations and day-to-day use.

Appendix D: Glossary of Terms (Excel Online, Office Scripts, Power Automate, etc.)

As you've explored modern Excel automation throughout this book, you've encountered many new tools, technologies, and terms. This glossary is designed to serve as a quick reference—not just for definitions, but for real-world understanding. Whether you're revisiting a concept or sharing this book with a colleague, this section will help demystify the language of automation and make the ecosystem easier to navigate.

Excel   Online

The web-based version of Microsoft Excel, accessible via browser through Microsoft 365. Excel Online supports collaboration, cloud storage via OneDrive or SharePoint, and is the platform where Office Scripts run. For example, a team working remotely across different time zones can simultaneously edit the same workbook without version conflicts.

Office   Scripts

A TypeScript-based scripting language designed for automating tasks in Excel Online. Office Scripts allow users to manipulate workbooks—read and write data, apply formatting, generate reports—without relying on desktop-only VBA macros. A typical script might clean up an imported data set, sort it, apply filters, and prepare a chart—all automatically.

Workbook

The main file type in Excel that contains one or more worksheets. In Office Scripts, the workbook object is the starting point for accessing sheets, tables, charts, and more. For example, workbook.getWorksheet("Summary") lets your script focus on a specific sheet.

Worksheet

A single tab or page within a workbook. You can read from or write to cells, manage formatting, or insert tables within a worksheet. A script might loop through all worksheets to summarize values into a dashboard.

Range   /   RangeArea

A range is a selection of one or more cells. In Office Scripts,

Range is used to work with continuous blocks, while
RangeArea can handle non-contiguous selections. For
instance, to set a title in cell A1, you'd use

```
getRange("A1").setValue("Monthly Sales").
```

Power   Automate
A Microsoft 365 service that allows users to create
automated workflows (called "flows") that connect apps and
services. Power Automate can trigger Office Scripts based
on events—such as when a file is created in SharePoint or
a form is submitted. A flow might collect survey responses
and run a script to update a tracking spreadsheet.

Connector
A service that links two systems in Power Automate. Excel
Online, SharePoint, Teams, and Outlook are all examples of
connectors. For example, the Excel connector can retrieve
data from a workbook, then pass it to Power BI for reporting.

Trigger
The event that starts a Power Automate flow. Triggers can
be time-based (e.g., every Monday at 8 a.m.) or action-
based (e.g., when a new file is added to a folder). A common
trigger might launch a flow every time a form response is
submitted.

Action
A step in a Power Automate flow that performs an
operation—such as running an Office Script, sending an
email, or updating a row in Excel. A flow might have multiple
actions that work together to build an end-to-end process.

Script   Lab
An add-in for Excel that allows you to experiment with
JavaScript or Office Scripts. It's useful for prototyping and
learning how different objects behave before deploying full
solutions.

Migrating VBA Macros to Office Scripts and Power Automate

TypeScript

The scripting language used to write Office Scripts. TypeScript is a superset of JavaScript and introduces typing and structure, making it easier to write reliable, maintainable code.

OneDrive / SharePoint

Cloud storage services that allow workbooks and scripts to be saved, shared, and accessed from anywhere. Office Scripts can only run on files stored in OneDrive or SharePoint, making them essential for cloud automation.

Flow Run History

A record of all executions of a Power Automate flow, showing when it ran, whether it succeeded, and where errors occurred. This log helps in troubleshooting and auditing automation performance.

Whether you're a business user, analyst, or Excel enthusiast, mastering this language of automation will help you communicate ideas more clearly, troubleshoot faster, and build smarter solutions. Keep this glossary close by— you'll likely refer to it as your automation projects grow in size and complexity.

Thank you for choosing and reading **Modern Excel Automation: Migrating VBA Macros to Office Scripts and Power Automate**. Your time, curiosity, and willingness to learn are what fuel innovation in the workplace. May this book serve as a launchpad for your own automation journey—one script, one flow, and one idea at a time.